A Year of Making and Learning

Designing Engaging Learning Experiences

Learning Connected

CONTENTS

Foreword

Why Learn by Making?

Dr William Rankin

Information is a modern invention.

That may seem odd or wrong, but it's absolutely true. Information as people often conceive of it — facts, numbers, abstract or generalised concepts, and data that has been removed from a specific context — all of this sort of "information" has only been around for a few hundred years, and it's certainly only been a focus of education for about that long. Before that, it didn't really exist for most people. In fact, organising and delineating that sort of information simply wasn't possible for most of human history. This is undoubtedly why the human brain is so bad at processing it.

Neuroscientists identify two main types of "declarative" or "explicit" memory — memory that we consciously store and retrieve: episodic memory and semantic memory. Episodic memory is tied closely to contexts and experiences, which is to say "episodes" in our lives. For example, remembering the way your grandparents made waffles — perhaps not only the techniques for beating and

1

folding in the egg whites, but also the experience of being with beloved family members — is a classic instance of episodic memory. Even years later as you remake the recipe, you'll likely recall the smell of the kitchen, the clink and heft of the yellow bowl your grandparents always used, and your pride and excitement at helping in the kitchen as you learned this particular culinary skill. In other words, your memory of how to make waffles is deeply connected to the context in which you learned it. It is less a collection of information and data and more a profoundly situated skill whose origins and persistence are deeply tied to specific episodes or experiences in your life.

Because of the richness of their context, these types of episodic memory can be created and stored quickly — and also quickly and easily retrieved, even years later. In some cases, episodic memory is so efficient that it can be created in a single instance, and it often takes only a handful of experiences for episodic memories to be permanently stored for later recollection.

With semantic memory, on the other hand, it's a much tougher slog. Semantic memories involve the memorisation of information as we often conceive it: decontextualised data and concepts that we must consciously work to memorise using lists, flash cards, worksheets, and repeated exercises. The quadratic formula memorised as an abstract equation with placeholder variables, the capitals of the countries in South America, the three classical rhetorical appeals, the sequence of geological or historical eras, and the elements and order of the periodic table are all instances of semantic information.

The problem is that human brains are very bad at processing and storing this sort of information. According to a number of recent neurological studies, but popularised in Dr John Medina's Brain Rules, when we're learning, the human brain can only hold around seven pieces of semantic information at any given time — and then we can do so for only about 30 seconds. When someone tells us a phone number, for example (a random collection of digits that we have to memorise first in order to associate them with that person), the first thing we have to do is start repeating them, at least until we can find a way to write them down. We repeat them because it's the only strategy most human brains have for holding onto this sort of information. And it gets worse. If we can't find a piece of paper, it will take much more repetition to move that information from working memory to short-term memory and from short-term memory to long-term memory. Much more. Not just seconds, not just minutes, not just hours, days, or months. In fact, according to recent studies, it will take about ten years of regular repetition for that kind of semantic information to become so entrenched in our memory that we don't lose it.

Don't believe me? Consider this: most people can remember their childhood telephone numbers or home addresses and rattle them off with hardly a thought. That's because for most of us, this information didn't change throughout our childhood and we had to use it repeatedly for more than a decade. But try to remember the phone number or address of your first job or that person you dated for a couple of years but eventually split from and you're likely to come up empty — even if you used to be able to repeat that information without thinking. I'm not even going to ask about that social media password you keep forgetting. Why do you lose your ability to recall this kind of information even though you were once so fluent? The ten-year rule. Yet if this is the case, then there's another question we have to ask. Why does semantic information take so long for us to remember? In other words, why is the human brain so bad at memorising this kind of information?

Because semantic information is a modern invention.

For most of human history, it was impossible for us to separate information from contexts and experiences. We simply didn't have enough control over our environments to pull that off. To make information semantic, we have to extract it from the environment and generalise it. That's no easy task, often requiring significant groundwork and resources to be in place before we can even try. More than that, it didn't make sense to abstract information in such a way for most people. We didn't need abstracted, generalised, decontextualised information: the contexts and experiences in which the information was embedded were often the most important aspect of that information for most people. For example, my maternal grandfather, a farmer who came from a line of farmers that stretched back at least 9 generations (and likely, well beyond that) could tell with uncanny accuracy that rain was coming two or three days before it actually arrived. He didn't do so by having memorised an abstract formula. He did so by having a deeply embedded experience of the place where he and his ancestors lived and by perceiving a complex and interconnected web of contextual cues: the behaviours of certain plants and insects, the colour of clouds at sunrise and sunset, the presence of dew on the morning grass, the smell and even the "feel" of the air. How did he learn this skill? By living in and experiencing a context for which such a perception was vital — and by being guided by others who had similarly learned this skill and for whom it was also equally vital. In other words, semantic information was far less useful for him than episodic information. And this was true for most humans on the planet for most of human history because most of us worked in trades or agriculture and learned not in schools but in apprenticeships and family groups. For most of human history, information was deeply and necessarily embedded in contexts.

That's precisely why semantic information presents such a challenge. Since it's effectively a recent invention, our brains simply haven't gotten good at managing and processing it yet. In other words, human brains were built for the episodic. They're better at processing it. And they prefer it. Semantic information doesn't come close.

Which is why it's so fascinating not only that formal education is often dominated by the semantic, but that the culture of standardised testing that emerged following the Second World War has doubled down on this form of information. Schools often require learners to drill intensively on subjects comprised almost exclusively of semantic information for a few months — if they're lucky, maybe even for the better part of a year — so they can pass a test that "proves" their learning. Thankfully, the majority of learners are able to provide this proof — which means governments, parents, and accrediting bodies can breathe a sigh of relief. Which they often do, despite the fact that learners are about nine years short of actually learning the information those tests are supposed to measure. Most of these learners' "learning" will evaporate faster than the July morning dew my grandfather would have looked for.

Of course, all of this shouldn't come as a surprise to anyone. Ask most parents, teachers, school administrators, or government officials to recite much of the vast amount of information they studied in school and were once able to pass tests on, and if it's not directly tied to their current work or lives, they won't be able to do it. Most people have lost most of the content — the facts and information — they "learned" over the dozen or more years they were in school. Sure, they still remember most of the basic skills, but the central information of most of their courses has faded away. Even more starkly, let a child ask a parent's help with homework in one of those topics — algebra, chemistry, literature, history, civics, etc. — and just watch the look of terror spread across that parent's face. It's the embodiment of that nightmarish experience of recognising a few details in a world that was once familiar and is now unrecognisable, the look of travellers in a foreign country who recognise a word or two but can do nothing to understand or make themselves understood.

It's time for this sort of wasteful nonsense to stop.

Since we know episodic memory is far more accessible for people and since schools honestly don't have (or don't take) the time to serve semantic information effectively to learners, we need a different approach.

The accounts you'll find in this book reflect the efforts of teachers all over the world to do just that. By embracing learning-by-making, these teachers are working to stop the wasteful dissipation of their learners' time and energies. By asking their learners to recognise problems, build solutions, and collaborate with others to produce rather than merely to consume, they're helping their learners develop an important set of "fusion skills" that will be essential for their ongoing success: collaboration, critical and design thinking, iteration, research and media literacy, creativity, and communication skills. More importantly, they're designing and creating the rich contexts necessary to spark and develop episodic memory for their learners, giving them ways to learn that are about passing far beyond a test rather than just passing it.

7

Most importantly, either tacitly or overtly, these teachers are acknowledging an important truth. Because while human brains are exceptionally inefficient at storing and retrieving semantic information, this is the chief capability of digital technologies. Rather than creating a generation of information-memorisers who can — and will — be easily replaced by machines, these teachers are trying to unleash something essential and vital in their learners: human creativity, human collaboration, and human dignity. The future doesn't belong to people who can memorise a list of decontextualised information. It belongs to people who understand profoundly how context shapes and changes information, who know how to read complex webs of interrelationships and interdependencies, and who can use these skills to decompose a problem; think critically about how to solve it; develop, test, and troubleshoot possible solutions; and work productively with others to make and enact change.

In other words, these teachers are reaching back beyond the newfangled concept of semantic information to recover something much older and much more powerful: a generation of people deeply connected to one another, to their environments, and to our world.

Introduction

Farida Danmeri

This book is ambitiously titled 'A Year of Making and Learning', not because it provides educational stories that took place in a specific year, but because it is hoped the stories will inspire readers to make this year a learning and making one no matter their context or experience. Why? Because considerable research suggests that impactful learning occurs when learners construct new knowledge through creating and sharing learning artefacts, such as a model, report or song. This student-centred approach to learning is also known as 'constructionism'.

This book does not claim to provide a 'perfect' approach to teaching and learning or a quick fix for improving education worldwide (because neither exists). Instead, it empowers educators to reflect on their teaching practice and identify how they can bring about deeper learning experiences for the learners they serve. How? Transformational learning occurs when we critically reflect on our experiences and those of others. This book draws upon the diverse voices and perspectives of twenty-four educators from fifteen countries across five continents with varied professional experience in primary through to tertiary education - in formal, non-formal and informal learning environments. It is hoped that the stories will catalyse the transfer of purposeful knowledge across geographic and cultural borders, expose educators to new ideas, and inspire them to take action to design impactful learning experiences wherever they are in the world.

Many books already exist on learning and making so how is this book different? This book does not provide educators with a checklist of how to replicate each educational story. Instead, it shares case studies of authentic learner-centred activities that can be adapted to your context. The stories have been written to provide enough structure to guide facilitators in how to deliver purposeful learning experiences but are loose enough to allow them to introduce their own ideas.

This book is divided into twenty international educational stories which address the points below in no fixed order:

- What was tried and the planning involved;
- Why this approach was tried and practical considerations;
- Key observations and results; and
- Recommendations.

As you read each educational story, I encourage you to highlight any ideas that you have not tried in your teaching practice. Afterwards, start brainstorming a few ideas on how you can incorporate them in your setting. It is up to you how many educational stories you would like to explore and conduct this exercise with. Once you have identified an idea to focus on, start to design your own learner-centred activity and trial it with your learners. Please do not put too much pressure on yourself to deliver an outstanding learning experience with your new idea. What works in one context, might not work in another. Instead, reflect on what you learned from the experience, what worked and how you could further develop the activity to support the progress of your learners. This book is an invitation for you to discover yourself as an educator and benefit your learners.

Chapter 1

Implementing P4C in the Secondary Classroom

Anita Jantunen

Pedagogical freedom is important for Finnish teachers. It is said to be one of the reasons why Finnish education has such a good reputation. Trying different pedagogical approaches is generally encouraged and the National Core Curriculum for Basic Education forms guidelines and defines contents and values but does not determine precisely how a teacher should teach. Finnish teachers are trusted to make the best possible pedagogical choices for their subject matter based on the group of learners. It also gives a great deal of power and influence to the teacher. Regarding ethics as a subject, it is important to have a safe atmosphere and a feeling of trust in the group as talking about life questions is sensitive. Sometimes it helps to take the focus away from the students and choose a more teacher-centred method, but it is not as effective for the learning process.

The latest core curriculum[1] from 2014 is said to be the biggest reform in Finnish education since the 1970s, when the comprehensive school system was founded.[2] The curriculum emphasises phenomenon-based learning, multidisciplinary learning, and transversal competences. The National Core Curriculum is based on a conception of learning that sees the students as active actors. The National Core Curriculum is a binding document and, along with the law, about the only limiting factor. Money and other resources also set limitations but if a teacher wants to try out a new pedagogical method which is supported by the curriculum, is not illegal or dangerous, and does not cost any extra, it can be done through pedagogical freedom without asking for permission or any need for justification. That is how I proceeded. I was inspired by a colleague of mine who is specialised in phenomenon-based learning while studying to become a classroom teacher in university. She was giving an introduction about the method in a meeting and it really made sense to me. I wanted to try it out as quickly as possible. I decided to do my experiment with 9th-graders (15-year-olds) as they were the oldest students in the school and have gained the most experience about learning. The experiment went so well that I used the same method for a completely different topic for 8th-graders the following year.

The course about ethics is taught to 9th-graders and is my personal favourite to teach. Young people are generally interested in discussions about life questions, which is both enjoyable and rewarding for a teacher. What bothered me was the setting where I selected the topics and the angle from which we approached different themes. I am an adult, I spent my middle school years without social media, my mobile phone was saved for very expensive phone calls only, and the internet was something that only 'nerds' managed. I can see the world of today's teenagers, but I do not have any lived experience in it. During my very first years in teaching, I enjoyed having control and power over what happened in the classroom. However, as I started to become a teacher (it is said to take approximately five years) I realised it was not about me at all - neither my power or preferences nor me knowing better. Recently, I have studied leadership and many of the principles related to leading others apply to the teaching profession. My role as a teacher is not to gain status or attention, but to serve. I am there for my students to assist and guide, encourage and support them.

Assessment of this type of subject always raises questions among students, a common question is, "Do I assess their opinions?" While this is not the case, I have explained it is about the thinking skills we are trying to develop. According to the National Core Curriculum, the emphasis is on assessment that promotes learning. Assessment culture should be a dialogical and interactive way of working that promotes the participation of pupils. One of the objectives of assessment is that the pupils are guided to make observations of their personal and shared work and to give constructive feedback to each other and the teachers. Developing assessment has been one of my personal interests and something I wanted to pay attention to, to make it ethical and fair.

I divided the course into two parts: the first part in the fall semester was about the ethical and moral theories and defining the concepts and learning to speak the language of ethics. I used the methods of Philosophy for Children (P4C)[3] to teach students to think philosophically. The second part was in the spring semester and focused on ethical questions, such as the beginning and end of life, environmental issues, drugs, animal rights, the rich and poor etc. It is an application of what is learned in the first part. One 45-minute lesson per week is scheduled for ethics, so there was not enough time to go through everything properly and choices needed to be made. I wanted to take a step (or a leap) towards more student-centred learning. Encouraged by the new curriculum and my previous positive experiences, I decided to try something different for the second part of the course.

The methods I had been using were basic phenomenon-based learning methods. I had a total of four parallel study groups to teach and I proceeded in the same way with each. In the first lesson after Christmas break, I wrote 'LIFE' (a phenomenon we were going to learn about) on a blackboard and handed out several post-it notes to every student. I asked them to write whatever came to their mind, something and anything that belonged to life, and to put the note on the board. While they read each other's notes, students came up with new things. After 20 minutes the blackboard was almost covered with notes. We looked through the words together and I asked the students to come and arrange the words into categories, so that the same type of words would be in the same category. The number of categories was not limited. This was the first lesson for me, as the students sorted the words differently than I would have done. At that moment, I also received proof of being on the right track. Sorted words were put in a safe place to wait for the next week.

In the second lesson, students were divided into smaller groups. Together we looked through the categories formed in the previous lesson and named them. I did some preparation and glued the notes on large papers which were now hung around the classroom. In those small groups, students took turns working with each category, giving suggestions as to: 1) what they found to be the most interesting topic(s) in that category, 2) what type of learning methods they would prefer when talking about this topic, and 3) how the learning process could be assessed. Each group had only a few minutes with each category, so it was a bit too fast-paced depending on the number of the formed categories.

In the third week, each small group was able to choose which category they would want to work with more closely. They had the suggestions the whole group had made and their task was to choose the topics which had gained most interest, decide which learning methods we were going to use (e.g. discussion, group work, posters, watching a documentary and reflecting, making art, making presentation), what are the learning objectives, and how the learning process is assessed. This could be continued at home if they ran out of time during the class. In the fourth week, they presented their ideas to the whole group and received feedback, and we created a schedule for the topics and assessment. We used a mobile application called SeeSaw[4] to create a communication and sharing platform for each group.

As a teacher, it is sometimes difficult to let go and let someone else take control, but with students I have a responsibility to follow their learning, so I demanded two things: during the upcoming two to three months, I wanted them to: 1) follow ethical issues in the media and 2) post their findings with a question or a thought to the SeeSaw group. This was mainly voluntary, and some were more active than others, but the use of a mobile app made it easy and fun, and it reached everyone. Another thing I asked them to do was to keep a learning journal. Some wanted to write by hand, so I gave them notebooks. Some wanted to write with a computer (which is also acceptable). Some students asked to do a vlog (why not!), another wanted to draw a comic and so on. All I wanted was to see that they thought about and processed what they had learned. During the last week of school before final grading, I had a discussion with every student based on the individual learning journals.

The feedback from the students was very positive. It is obvious that there are always one or two who have a certain attitude towards school or a single subject and would rather be somewhere else, but while observing the class in the individual discussions and the feedback, I collected the students who were committed, motivated, and developed as philosophical thinkers. They said they especially liked that the learning methods varied, the topics felt meaningful, there were no tests, and the learning objectives were clear.

As a teacher, this was a very pleasant experiment. In the beginning of February, all the lessons for the whole spring for 9th-graders were planned by the students. I only needed to do some preparation work. Some of the methods required cooperation with another teacher. For example, if we were to explore a forest to think about our relationship with nature, I needed some help from a biology teacher on where to go. I also asked an art teacher when we were to paint or photograph about love and friendship.

Ethics passes through almost every subject in school and it is easy to integrate to match many topics even though it is not taught as a separate subject. I highly encourage all teachers to discuss life questions, good and bad, and right and wrong with their students. More importantly, I encourage them to listen to their students and ask questions. What I learned from this experience is that a student-centred approach makes learning more meaningful and enhances learning. Students appreciate when they are treated as individuals and listened to. Support from the core curriculum encouraged me to abandon traditional tests and concentrate on the learning process. It did not matter that parallel groups had slightly different learning content, methods, and objectives as all the groups focused on ethical topics and developed as learners and philosophers. Is there any harm if one group wants to learn more about war and peace and the other one about refugees?

In our world, regardless of where we live, it is crucial to be able to think, especially critically. Social media and mobile technology are affecting our brains and not only in a good way. In my opinion, critical and ethical thinking, empathy, and imagination are the keys to success in life in the future as they are the human features that a machine cannot replace.

Chapter 2

Developing Self-Learning Communities to Promote Social and Tech Innovations in Making

Xavier Auffret, Romain Chanut and Justine Hannequin

The Jerry computer can was born at the French National School for Advanced Studies in Design (ENSCI), Paris in 2011. The first one was designed by Xavier Auffret, Chemsedine Herriche, and Laure Guillou. The Jerry is a computer that is easy to make with second-hand materials that are commonly regarded as waste items. We aimed to make computer science more accessible and affordable to all by recycling easily obtainable cheap materials, such as a jerrycan. What we designed is a system that:

- Makes a computer simple to build for everybody (using easy-to-find materials that can be assembled).

- Makes informatics look simple using simple objects from daily life as raw materials: the use of a jerrycan as a body for a computer changes the way you approach informatics by making you feel that it is not that complicated! The Jerry is the opposite of a black box computer.

- Makes learning fun and customisable.

According to us, Jerry's original and simple shape is a big part of its success: it generated a lot of curiosity and made many people willing to "get their hands dirty" with informatics. The Jerry was successful in several countries. The first collective workshop took place in France in March 2012, the Ivory Coast in May, then Benin, Togo and Algeria in the following months. Then ten more French-speaking countries in West Africa contacted us. The quick success happened for a mixture of reasons. We have strong values based on free software and hacker ethics, so we had strong connections with people who shared the same values. Jerry is a tangible product, so people can take and share pictures to show the results of their work, which does not work with software code at the core of Linux communities. In developing countries, access to hardware is much more expensive and the hardware products are much more likely to break than in northern countries, where they are designed. The local context of tropical countries is not considered by IT industrial players. In any case, we had substantial feedback showing curiosity about the first Jerry, the one we now call 'the mothership', as it is the origin of a multitude of Jerry's children.

The DIY approach enables fast replication. The length of time to create the Jerry, however, depends on the local needs and the resources available: as the local community of contributors crowdsource everything, timing is extensible. If you have the proper components and you just want a regular computer with an end-user operating system, you can assemble your Jerry computer within four to six hours. If you want a more complex design and/or specific software solution, it could be a week of work to get the result you expect.

We wanted to go beyond our original aim of making informatics more accessible with each Jerry computer. We quickly realised that one of the real challenges was to make all innovations accessible to the global community. Indeed, even if Jerry was quite easy to assemble, there would not be many Jerry computers built without a community of contributors. We focused on listening to and discussing with potential contributors to effectively develop our international community. As Jerry began to receive interest from people, we started to send them pictures and shared our first 'how-to' guide. The idea was to help them to build their own Jerry but also share feedback from others within the community. This enabled them to improve their own Jerry whilst sharing improvements with the community to start a virtuous circle. As Jerry first spread around Europe and then later around the world, the name 'JerryClan' naturally emerged. Local volunteers in French-speaking African countries felt a strong sense of values around ecology, transparency, and free software ethical issues.

Finally, the mothership was a starter model that triggered curiosity and contributed towards the development of our sharing philosophy. This made the transformation of concrete projects by people living in remote areas possible. We also wrote a manifesto very quickly which compiled all the values that seemed important to us; it was a way for us to explain who we were and strengthened our relationships with people from around the world who shared common values. In 2013, there were ten active JerryClan communities around the world. We realised that we had an issue around documenting and bringing all initiatives of the community together. That is why we developed a documentation platform where you are invited to register your Jerry.[5] By doing so, contributors share their knowledge and inspire the next generation of contributors.

Many improvements on Jerry are coming from the community. One example is the way of closing Jerry: the first generation of Jerry computers was attached with a zipper that had to be sewn. It is beautiful and it closes Jerry very properly, but it also involves a lot of work! We experimented with new closing systems and managed to reduce the working time. There are plenty of other examples of improvements coming from this collective approach: a new way of making hinges was also invented, different fixing solutions, etc. Quickly, Jerry Do It Together became a global movement powered by hundreds of people around 14 countries. There is no 'Jerry Office' and nobody is employed by 'Jerry Corp', so the movement has remained organic since its beginning. It also means that we cannot predict the future because every day a new step is made in an existing or new direction. Each local community JerryClan is fully self-organised. Specific economic models (technical support) and disruptive innovations (healthcare SMS-based application) emerged from the Jerry infrastructure and specific local needs and resources. For example, in Tchad, the cultural French centre wants to share Internet access with the locals, but there is no computer available. The JerryClan Tchad built more than ten Jerry Computers for the French cultural centre, so people can connect on the Internet and use web services. However, these Jerry computers must be maintained to support their access to the Internet. So, the JerryClan Tchad became the IT operator of this cyber room, providing care for the machines and the software they host.

Another brilliant example is the SMS based application hosted on a Jerry computer. Developers and hackers from the Ivory Coast had the idea to connect a mobile phone to the Jerry. This Jerry is a server (which means its role is to 'serve' other devices) and hosts SMS applications that are designed to answer specific needs. For example, Mpregnancy is dedicated to pregnant women who cannot access a doctor but who need medical advice. These women are invited to send their body temperature once a week by SMS to the Jerry server. If the result is not appropriate, the doctor will receive a notification by SMS so he or she can call the female patient.

The Jerry has been extensively used in educational contexts. According to Romain Chanut, one of the most memorable educational projects was an early event in 2012 held in Algeria. We organised a two-week workshop in Algeria at the Higher National School of Computer Science (ESI) and the University of Science and Technology Houari Boumediene. We created a very detailed Facebook event to maximise the information available for potential attendees and to enable online word-of-mouth. We are very inspired by the SCRUM / agile methodologies to enable attendees to self-organise. We set a general objective - building a functional and beautiful Jerry computer - and attendees were invited to express all the actions/requirements they imagined. Then, each attendee chose one action and became responsible for the execution for the next sprint, working in pairs to keep creativity up and not be stuck on their own on a problem. We were invited by a local association, so we designed the workshop depending on the needs of the students (refer to the process diagram for more information about the workshop design). In the long-term, there is always the question of economic incentive: fully volunteered initiatives can make wonderful things emerge but maintaining in the long-term requires consistent resources, not only good will.

We did our best to answer the very basic questions that everybody wanted to access. We developed the project with their engagement in mind. It was important for us to know who was participating. From this, we were able to plan what they would do, how we would proceed, and when and where the event would be delivered. We also had public presentations at the university to present the workshop to students so they would know what to expect.

The local young crowd made the Facebook event rapidly viral (400 virtual attendees). Thanks to that, we got the attention of local media. We got one national TV channel coverage and at least four articles in major newspapers. We identified a general pattern that can be observed for any web-based citizen-powered initiative: online actions prepare effective 'real-life' gatherings. The story of the real-life gathering is shared online so that potential contributors can see how the collective movement is shaping. Then, new contributors have enough knowledge and trust to make the decision to act.

Another interesting point about the pedagogical potential of the Jerry is how we can use it for multiple workshop formats and diverse subjects. Finally, very often we use Jerry's just to spark conversation about informatics and introduce some relevant issues. For example, in many workshops we disassemble computers, smartphones, etc with participants to show everyone what is inside a computer and how complicated it is to reassemble. A computer is a very complex object because of its modernity. We can spend days explaining how the various parts of the machines were built and what the relationships are between the components, how they are complementary etc, however, the purposefulness of such an exercise is questionable. The ultimate goal is for the Jerry to have a positive impact on the community and to encourage people to shape new habits inspired by the creative and innovative process in developing the tool.

Chapter 3

Developing International Networks of Innovation

David Li

I started Xinchejian, the first makerspace in China, while living in Shanghai. It is essentially a hobbyist space. In 2011, with two collaborators from the University of Michigan and NYU Shanghai, we started to think about the maker movement. We are all big fans of the cyberpunk genre, which contributed towards the development of SZOIL. We were really interested in bottom-up technical driven innovations - they fascinated us. Originally, we set up to look at how the maker movement was going to impact on the mass production ecosystem in China and our research took us everywhere. In 2010, I noticed the interests of makers started to pick up. We were invited to talk at many events because of Chris Anderson's book. Usually, when they publish a book on the maker movement, you must mention open source where people generously share all their projects with the community. Most places I am invited to talk at want me to discuss this topic. Typically, the first question I am asked is if we share everything and open source everything, how do you make money?

I have been involved in open source software since 1990. This is a kind of new economic model. Back in 2011, I gave a talk in Shenzhen. After my talk, I was ready to answer that question. But the question from my audience was instead, well, what's new? We have been doing business like this for 20 years. What's new about this? That interaction really triggered our interest in what else has been happening in Shenzhen. Importantly, why does everybody else have that reactionary question about how openness is not a money-making opportunity? We took our research forwards to really investigate what's going on in Shenzhen and how that experience can inform the maker movement.

We are still running the makerspace. We were involved in the maker faire. We did a programme for the maker faire in Shenzhen in 2012 and 2013. We continued to do a lot of this research, such as interviews and surveys - everything. Then we published about our learning in Shenzhen. Some of the reports are associated with the Shenzhen government. In 2015, I was offered a grant to start a makerspace, which is where the Shenzhen Open Innovations Lab came from. We decided it would be a fablab as well. Our engagement with the entire network is somewhat different. We see SZOIL as the bridge between the ideas generation's fab lab network and production-driven Shenzhen. The goal is to figure out how to bring those two together. Shenzhen has a history of being a centre of development. This has contributed greatly to the maker movement. Everything can be made cheaply here. Many factories here are using laser cutters, and the entire infrastructure lowers the cost of the machine so that the makerspace can get started.

We started the makerspace, during the year of 2010, it was not intended to make money; it was intended for pleasure and recreation. A group of 12 people could afford to buy a laser cutter. We want to help makers everywhere. When they go into a makerspace, they learn about electronics and what they can do with them. When they are ready, they can come and start to scale. It would be strange for us to set up a fablab in the middle of Shenzhen, saying, now we are going to teach you how to manufacture. We are there to help.

The entire economy of Shenzhen is manufacturing. That informs the thinking behind what the maker movement means. The maker movement is really for the people. Education is important. It enlightens people and develops their skills in electronics. Now I can take these electronics into a tool kit to help solve problems. In 2014, we kicked off the fablab by hosting the festival. Every year there is a big gathering of people from fablabs. In 2011, it was in Boston. When we opened our fablab, we also hosted the festival. It was a good event. 1000 people came from around 130 fablabs from 76 countries from all over the world. We wanted to connect Shenzhen to the world. We have started to think of Shenzhen as a resource: open, collaborative, sharing, just like a makerspace, so we started to reach out to makerspaces from around the world. However, we did not network much in China.

We set up to be a global platform. Our actions have been informed by research and the research is really supporting the idea that we need to empower more people to be able to build stuff and commercialise it. The makerspace is a place for education, empowerment and development. We want to show people how to leverage a maker space prototype. We aim to send them to the next point. We did not engage much domestically as many makerspaces are doing it already. We decided to develop our international relationships. That is one of the reasons we are part of the fablab network.

When we first set up an international project, we set out to engage with mostly the US west coast, Silicon Valley, makerspaces, incubators and accelerators. We found the US side does not really match well with what Shenzhen represented. One side of US making is this free-thinking, hippie culture of self-expression. They did not make products. The entrepreneurs are all about evaluation. It is never about making real products. We engaged with Europe and the British Council in 2016. We launched a programme called the Hello Shenzhen centre.[6] In 2016, we sent British makers to Shenzhen and Shenzhen makers to the UK for a four-week exchange. That was the biggest event for the British Council that year and it was also the most popular event for the British Council. It was very fun. There was generally a lot of exchange of information and data. We developed our maker network in Amsterdam, Berlin, and Paris. I think European makers have their heart in the right place, but their speed of production is just too slow for us. Making a hardware product is not a permanent installation. It is an 18-month upgrading cycle. You're never going to launch to the public so you must get to the market fast to make your impact and make your money. You need something for you to go on with and you cannot spend three years (half your time) making the project, and the other half of your time making grant applications.

Because of those factors, we started to link up to makerspaces in Africa. Right now, we have a network across Ethiopia, Kenya, Ghana, and Nigeria. We are also helping projects in Somalia in Djibouti. The fun part was realising that the African makers are a perfect match for Shenzhen because the maker movement gives them the knowledge, courage, and education to use electronics or fabrication skills to do things. Looking around Africa, there are many issues. However, these also offer opportunities and many African fabbers that we worked with were coming to makerspaces with lots of ideas, or they go out there and find a paying customer and try to build their product as soon as possible. This is what we regard as the maker spirit: I come to a makerspace and I learn, now I can do things. Now let me use my skills to solve problems, for example the problems of my neighbours. We found that engagement very fulfilling and so we have been expanding throughout Africa. During 2017 and 2018, great effort was put in developing our partnership in Africa. One thing we did last year with the support of the Ministry of Science and strategy of Ethiopia was to launch a maker exchange programme. Now we are supporting the founders on that side. It grows as a competition or hackathon training. 9000 people across Ethiopia signed up. For the final five teams selected, we had five makers from Shenzhen to go there, deliver training and now the top five projects are out for the past two productions.

A three-person team in Somalia is currently launching their own mobile phone, while another is launching in Djibouti. We are also engaging with some of the urban mobility projects in Nairobi. In Ghana, there's a lot of work with small farming projects. We are looking at the makerspace narrative because it is linked to Dale Dougherty, the US east coast narrative, and the MIT fablab. It is about coming and becoming exceptional, coming and changing the world. Considering Shenzhen, this is the empowerment narrative, the maker movement should be empowering ordinary people to understand what they can do and then going out and doing something. It does not matter whether it is big or small. There is the above-mentioned three-person team in Somalia, trying to develop mobile phone services through their new mobile phone brand. Then someone gives a TED talk and so on. I would like our work to make an impact on everyone. Making an impact comes down to how many units you ship regardless of where your TED talk is. If you do not ship anything, you will not make an impact. What we would love to see is a bridge between gigantic maker cities. We would love to see how we could help more. We could see how we can help more children by teaching them, thus having a social and economic impact.

Chapter 4

Launching an EcoTecLab: Empowering Communities in Togo

Ousia Foli-Bebe

My journey as a maker and STEAM (science, technology, engineering, art, and maths) education activist started years ago. In fact, my dream was to design and produce clean technology and solutions for agriculture. I then studied renewable energies and later environment and life quality. My schoolmates and I were full of ideas but at school the learning was more theoretical. Most of the lectures did not link what we were learning to what we could do with it in real life. Sometimes it was frightening just to think that the next lecture would be mathematics - even in college. We then decided to start tinkering on our own. I had some tools already so we would meet at my place and build things. That led us to build and experiment with a solar cooker, earth battery, a small windmill recycling computer hard drives. Later, I decided to start building and prototyping clean solutions for agriculture and joined a local fablab. It was not really the maker experience I was looking for plus it was difficult to find people to help build solutions to specific problems with which they were presented. I then noticed the difficulty of finding somebody with maker/craftsman knowledge and the will or time to share and assist youths.

I then decided to start a makerspace. EcoTecLab started in a classroom with benches, the tools accumulated during my year of tinkering from high school, and the help and the passion of two colleagues - one from a renewable course I took and the other from an environmental course. The goal was simple: to prototype clean energy solutions for agriculture and empower the youth by developing practical skills to build and assist people who found themselves in the same position as I did during my early fablab experience. For us, being a makerspace and not a fablab in our context is important to assist and involve local craftsmen and empower people to create useful innovations. A fablab can sometimes focus solely on digital fabrication which is not necessarily appropriate for an African context.

Fablabs usually consist of the following three main components: a makerspace, co-working space, and a start-up incubator. Most of their activities are invested in the co-working and incubation aspects, leading to fewer hands-on activities. However, in the same DIY and sharing spirit, I found fablabs to be less inclusive for our African craftsmen who are often not computer literate at all. To overcome this barrier, we need to involve the craftsmen and help them build tech and computing skills. This can be done through providing a space with tools they know and use every day where they can learn step-by-step how to use computer-aided design (CAD) or electric tools. Craftsmen and participants can then slowly transition from operating hand tools to electric tools and digital fabrication and prototyping. Also, leading young innovators through those steps allows them to understand the challenges of craftsmen. They can then work together on innovative and more inclusive solutions.

Since making and hand-crafting activities are very important in our makerspace, we do open making workshops. These events are open to everybody: makers, non-makers, students, craftsmen, engineers and beyond. Every last Saturday of the month we host making workshops around topics like solar oven-making, wind gauge-making, e-waste made 3D printers, etc. For each topic, we do a design thinking section together with all the participants. We decide how to build it, the steps required, and then start building it together. Mostly, participants do not know how to use some tools so we assist them while delegating responsibilities. This helps participants develop their design thinking skills and learn from others. Participants that are new to making learn a lot about the topic in one section. They find the topic demystified and sometimes learn more about what they already know. We make them understand why or how the actual making topic is related to them even if they are not from that field. They then discover a new passion, learn new ways of doing things, and find solutions to some issues they may be facing.

Together with public workshops, we made the most of our furniture and 3D printer.

Later in 2017, we were involved in the building of a mobile STEAM lab: The molab project.[6] It began with a call for a design proposal from the US Embassy in Togo. We proposed a design and it was selected. We then built it, equipped it with solar panels, a 3D printer, computers, creative and construction-based games and books in both French and English. The molab team members were from diverse fields. We travel from school to school around the country. Our team aims to spark genius and inspire and motivate young people to be solutions providers for our communities and global challenges.

We go to a remote area where schools are not usually in concrete and sometimes lack infrastructure and electricity. Our molab allows children to see a 3D printer in action. They can see a 3D printed robot, do experiments, look through a microscope, enjoy science through music, and understand how they can be a solution to local problems in their community.

The molab team consists of an artist, a biologist, an English teacher, a creative and building game animator and of course makers. As a maker, my role is to facilitate tinkering workshops, such as robotics, technology, and 3D printing to inspire young people. I do this by linking my workshop to what they learn in school like maths, physics, biology etc and getting them involved in the process. The molab is open to all members of the community, however, our key target group is young people. Adults from the local community also collaborate with us to facilitate workshops.

For example, in robotics we show them and play with a robot we made at the EcoTecLab.[7] First, I ask them what it is or looks like when I show them the robot spider. After getting answers like "it looks like a crab or spider" and "it is a robot or a machine", we also discuss the origin of the robot. Most of them answer that it is made in Africa, and some or few will say Togo. It is an important step to stress the necessity for them to have a sense of observation and analysis in life. We exercise this by encouraging them to observe a crab or a spider, understand how it walks, and to build a machine that looks like one. I then tell them it is made locally in Togo and they can also make it using what they have been studying in school.

We then identify key parts together, discussing what the arms and motors could be made of. We then design a robotic arm for a physically impaired person in their community. They discuss what a human arm is made of (bones, muscles, joints, cartilage etc). They then compare the robot's arm to their own and discuss how they could make a joint using motors. We also expand upon the notions in biology they have just used to identify structures of their arms. We then draw an arm on the board and discuss and continue designing the robot arm using notions like angle and later code for that arm, such as an action like a military salute. After such sessions, they understand and can relate the control board on the robot to their brain. They create connections between my cell phone communicating with the robot and communication with humans. They understand that for this robot to be created, many people must come together to share their expertise. Innovation, technology, and techniques are put together. This is a way of showing the pupils their uniqueness and empowering them to work together for innovation and progress.

We conclude with question and discussions. We discuss the fact they are unique and the importance of the fact that they are being solution providers in their community. During discussions, I often relate to other Togolese innovators like Mr Logou who made the FouFouMix, which is a machine to help make an African meal called 'Fufu'. Fufu is made by pounding yams. It tastes good but it is not easy to make because of the difficulty in manually pounding yams. I link this to the importance for them to develop their sense of observation and analysis as mentioned earlier so they can create useful innovations for their community and the world. I share with them the importance of having goals and perseverance to thrive in life. During goal setting activities, I empower then to start thinking of what they want their legacy to be to the world. They learn that by having goals, they can develop them and expand on expertise in a field of interest through searching on the internet and engaging in self-learning.

Through Thomas Edison's story of inventing the light bulb, I empower them to persevere and never give up. Sometimes their teachers even relate this story to their homework, to help them when they unsuccessfully try to do their maths or physics homework, or asking questions to understand the lesson.

Although this educational project has been successful, it must be sustainable and continue to develop. As a farmer plants a seed, it must be taken care of until it reaches maturity. We must keep the STEAM empowerment going with these children, which is why on our tours we empower them to set up science clubs. We also offer our assistance in keeping it running through advice, discussing events they can organise, or helping them in getting materials from the capital to their community schools. We also share a few experiments they can start using with local resources.

Looking forward, we are also working on a STEAM set that we can produce through funding and giving them to science clubs, so they keep going. The science set aims not only to do science experiments. We are designing it with a design thinking and problem-based learning approach to develop the critical thinking skills of participants. While it is important to empower youth through STEAM and tinkering, one should not neglect the leadership skills they can develop in the process. We must give them not only STEAM but the best of us as humans without pretending to be perfect.

Chapter 5

Investigating the Greatness of the Past

Camila Cerezo and Malena Cerezo

This project was delivered at the Instituto Esteban A. Gascón, a private primary school in Buenos Aires, Argentina.[8] It is an innovative and small school in the heart of the Palermo neighbourhood. 23 students from grade 4° were involved in this project. A special educational needs teacher collaborated with the class teacher and supported the learning of two students with special educational needs. The principal aim of our educational project was to spark students' curiosity and promote their engagement in the learning process.

In the Argentinean education system, the primary education curriculum initially allows for flexibility and is well thought-out, however, as the children grow it generally tends to become more restrictive and prescriptive. As the children progress through each grade, more importance is given to the accumulation of memorised facts than the process of learning itself. This gives the feeling that school experiences have not changed much over the past 20 years. In this particular school, the headmistress believes in experimenting with new approaches to teaching and learning. Due to the positive learning environment of this school, teachers feel comfortable with experimenting with unconventional teaching strategies. We planned and presented a unique history project design to the headmistress. She was very open to the idea and keen to support us in exploring different ways of delivering our project.

We often find the resistance to educational change comes from the parents of pupils. As an innovative school, we wanted to demonstrate that other ways of learning can be even more successful than those that have already been tried and tested in the past. Our teaching community was eager to explore novel ways of promoting meaningful learning experiences. As a result, we were motivated to collaborate and put these classes together. The planning and delivery of the classes sometimes involved two teachers working together. This approach is quite common in Argentina.

After a week of observing the classes and having two meetings with the headmistress, we identified the need for us to take content from the social sciences curriculum and incorporate it in other areas. This was because the students had less interest in this subject for some reason. We wanted to change their view on social sciences. The specific content was on the two great pre-Columbian empires of Central America: the Aztecs and the Mayans. When we traditionally think of history or other social sciences, sometimes it is hard to approach teaching and learning actively. How can we be a part of things that are in the past? How can we keep children motivated when we are talking about other cultures, sometimes far away from their own realities? We believe the answer could be found through developing the passion of students, trying to drive and maintain their motivation and take advantage of their curiosity. All the information about our topic could be found on the Internet. The key challenge for teachers today is to actively involve children in other's realities by linking them to things from everyday life that they already know.

To catch the attention of the students and share our 'new teaching' idea, we started the lesson with personal images of different travels from diverse contexts where those civilisations have developed. We wanted to share our own experiences and inquire about their possible contacts with these landscapes. Some of the children already knew areas of Mexico and had contact with the archaeological ruins. This was the first lesson; we used a PowerPoint slide projected on a big screen with different travelling pictures, some of them were very funny and others were casual. In those pictures they could see ruins, landscapes, architecture and sculptures. We talked about what they saw to investigate the students' prior knowledge by asking neutral questions. Examples include: "Where do you think those photos were taken?", "What landscape do you see?", "What are those ruins?", "Do people live there now?", "Why?", and "How might you know that?"

Afterwards, we searched the locations using Google Maps. Finally, we asked how they thought these ruins were discovered. Who were the professionals involved in this? Who did it? What could you find besides the ruins? What tools did they use? What other things might they find? They then remembered the Indiana Jones movies.

We watched two videos that explained the social structure of these two civilisations in a very interesting and funny way.[9] We then brainstormed our ideas in groups and organised them together in a chart to allow us to compare and contrast the Aztecs and Mayans. For example, we explored social organisation, location, economy, etc. We wanted to avoid a class that was purely discussion; we wanted students to demonstrate their learning through creating artefacts. We thought of an activity that would connect them with the Aztecs while creating an artefact that represented their learning journey. We knew that this group of pupils liked to paint so we gave them the activity of painting an Aztec calendar. They were so fascinated that they continued painting them - even in the playground. They called them the Aztec mandala, because they paint mandalas all the time, so they connected the new information with something familiar to them. The children were very interested in those warriors and of course the mysterious disappearance of the Mayans. They were very surprised about the technological developments of both ancient civilisations. They could not believe that some of our favourite foods were known to these ancient civilisations and were their favourite foods too. We made them popcorn and brought it to the class for them to try. They were very excited about it.

The second lesson was very different from our regular lessons. We created an interdisciplinary lesson - a Mesoamerican ball game by collaborating with the physical education teacher. The ball game was one of the ritual customs for both the Aztecs and Mayans. We discussed the similarities this game had with other games of our own culture, like football. We explained how the Aztecs and Mayans played it. The children concluded that the Aztecs and Mayans must have been very skilled people as playing the ball game was very difficult. We talked about the rules of the game. "What happened to those who made a goal?" "What if they won the game?" The children recognised the difficulty of the game, especially because of the great physical effort involved.

The class discussed new rules for playing it - they wrote them on a big piece of paper and hung it in the playground. We made four teams and started playing! The children had fun and suggested organising a small championship. So, we did. Still now, when we cross them in the playground, they ask us if we can organise a new championship. A passion for the sport was present in all members of the class.

In the last class, we worked with the maths and art teacher to develop a project where students built their own pyramids of Teotihuacan. We showed them two pyramids built by us, each one represented the pyramid of the sun and the moon.

The students were divided into groups of four. We gave them a set of paper shapes that make up a pyramid (one small square, one large square, and four equal parallelograms) and a large sheet where they could assemble all the pieces. With those pieces, they were to draw on the sheet so that a pyramid can be formed with a single piece of paper, folding and sticking it on one side only. Our pupils are used to working in groups; we find this encourages them to constantly exchange dialogue which develops their interpersonal skills. We conducted this activity outside of the classroom - something very common in our school.

The results were amazing. The children were so motivated and excited about the challenge that they created solutions faster than we thought they would. Only one group did not complete it in one piece. We encouraged them to reflect on how they could improve the pyramid-making process. They acknowledged that they all had different ideas and it was difficult to agree with each other. In the end, they built a pyramid, but it involved sticking more than one side. The groups mostly resolved it in the same way: the big square in the centre. One group thought differently. It was a challenge for us to identify quickly whether it worked. The pupils then tested their design by building one pyramid each. They then personalised their designs by decorating them. Some of the pupils asked for educational books to support them with this activity. We brought and shared different books about Aztecs and Mayans with the class. They wanted to be inspired by some of the existing images.

To finish the project, we each took a pyramid and assembled them in cardboard and clay. Next, we built the pyramid environment in pairs, so there was a pyramid of the sun and one of the moon, representing Tenochtitlan. Some of the works were exhibited in the school.

The overall experience was amazing for both the pupils and the teachers. The children were so excited that they were talking about the classes every time we encountered them. One of the things that caught their attention was when we were talking about the sacrificial rituals. The idea of the honour involved in sacrificing for the community was shocking for them. They then started to understand that different cultures could have different worldviews. It was interesting how we were able to link this subject to different subjects like maths, art, social science and gym. We believed that we could also relate the topic to Spanish, natural science and music. It is more interesting for children and more organic for a teacher to choose a whole theme and start to think about the different subjects involved. When we finished, we thought that maybe we could relate the topic to a Spanish class by studying the legend represented on the shield of the flag of Mexico. We also thought about our own legends. Maybe the children could create their own mythology stories. This mix between history and myths is one of the biggest imprints of pre-Columbian cultures - children find it fascinating.

In general, we think that any subject could be taught in this format. It is important first to know the group of children. In our case, we knew that they were very curious and enjoyed sharing ideas, which is why we started with something personal. We aimed to immediately capture their attention. This made it easier to engage them in the proposed activities and challenges. They felt like they were playing all the time: imagining, interacting, and creating. The experience was magnificent and did not require many materials. You can be innovative with some books, the internet, glue, paper and a ball - very simple things that you can find in any school. We presented students with contextual challenges to capture their attention and fuel their enthusiasm. They said the activities made them feel like Indiana Jones waiting for action!

The school asked us to share the project with our wider teaching community, so now all 4th grade students learn about Aztecs and Mayans in this manner. We are working with the teachers in this way, to find one common underlying theme that can be linked to the diverse learning needs of the students. The assignment is not easy at all. The teachers are often more focused on the content they are supposed to teach as opposed to the learning process. It was a great challenge to suggest the kind of classes we had designed. When children have a good time at school, teachers and parents approach it with scepticism. They ask, are they learning? But the children remember the content of the class too. They learn a lot about the ancient civilisations that lived in America before us. The most important thing is, they still want to know more about them. Is that not the major goal of primary school? To keep children yearning for more?

Here is some of the work they made:

Painting the Aztec calendar

Ball game rules

Painting the pyramids

Pyramids at the school's year exhibition

Chapter 6

Dance as a Multi-Sensory Approach to Learning

Alison Swann

At about this time last year, I was in school chatting to a Year 4 teacher. I was there working with all teachers, facilitating their professional development around using dance as a multi-sensory approach to learning, linked to and supporting other subject areas. The focus in Year 4 was mathematics. As we were discussing her plans, she said to me: "I cannot teach dance. I cannot keep time with music. I cannot count to it." She had a preconceived idea about what it was to teach dance - standing in front of the class, demonstrating a routine to the children and counting them in - five, six, seven, eight...and I knew I could show her another way.

Together, we continued to plan dance sessions linked to symmetry. After several weeks of me leading, then team teaching, and finally handing the class over to her, she realised that her fears were unfounded. She did not need to demonstrate dance in front of her class. She understood that it was about asking the right questions so that the children were free to explore dance and mathematical concepts in a creative, embodied and collaborative way.

51

That by framing challenges and instructions meant she became a facilitator rather than an instructor, she WAS able to teach dance, and dance became yet another tool for learning.

I am thrilled to say that we have kept in touch. She still uses this approach to teach and support a range of wider curriculum concepts.

In 2005, when I joined the Learning and Access team at The Place[10] to deliver professional development to teachers in primary schools, it was to be a part of what would culminate in 15 years of research[11] into embodied learning. I had been teaching dance in a cross-curricular way for some years, but as a dancer it is tempting to run away with an idea, or even leave it behind, whilst creating pleasing movement.

At The Place, our practice took on different forms over the years. Starting with, simply, 'Dancing the Words', it became 'Learn Physical' and then 'Learn Physical Interactive'. These programmes at The Place, and what I do now in schools across the country, goes beyond simply cross-curricular dance, or as I often describe it, dipping your toe into the curriculum for an idea. Using dance as a multi-sensory approach to learning is about embodying learning concepts through movement, breaking down and deconstructing subject language and giving access to scientific, mathematic, historical and other concepts to all children. It gives us stimuli for dance, and more importantly enriches learning in the broad sense. If we embody something, if we learn through doing and making dance, learning is deeper and longer-lasting. It quite literally is 'in our bodies'.

When I work in schools with children and with teachers, I make sure that I am fully aware and informed of what the children are learning in the classroom. Dance can only be effective in supporting the curriculum if we all use the same language. Over time, I have discovered that the primary curriculum is a rich source of dance stimuli. The basis for any education system is language. It is how we communicate with students, and how many lessons are delivered or facilitated. Language is where children often experience a barrier to learning. Using dance as a multi-sensory approach offers an alternative way of exploring learning and curriculum areas, embodying and gaining a deeper understanding of words and concepts.

Dance is about expressing a thought, feeling, or idea. Teaching dance in all age phases should focus on these three key concepts. Children should be encouraged to develop their ideas through structured, yet flexible lessons where they develop a vocabulary of movement.

I have found that teaching a particular style or genre of dance can therefore be restrictive, both to the teacher who has little or no experience but crucially to the children. Whilst there are very strong arguments for the teaching, study and appreciation of popular and cultural dance styles, focussing too much on any of these, particularly at primary level, can be divisive and comes with a risk of alienating most of the class. Children feel as though they 'cannot do it' or that they 'do not want to do it'. These issues often arise when children are taught routines in popular dance styles.

When I first started my training at Laban (now Trinity Laban), dance in schools was known as Modern Educational Dance. Looking back, I see that this was an apt description, as it suggests that this does not mean one particular style of dance. Instead, a dance specialist could at that time draw on their varied dance experience and that of the children to 'create' dance, and not to simply repeat a set of steps to perform a routine created by the teacher.

Dance can, and should, encourage students to create movement that helps them to solve problems and understand that thought, feeling, or idea used as a stimulus. The role of the teacher is to facilitate this, and not simply to ask them to copy us. Dance is an art, and is by its very nature, expressive. To reach the end of a lesson and have 30 children, or several groups of children, all perform the same thing, is anything but.

2018 marked the centenary of the end of the Great War. A school I work in regularly had this as a focus throughout the school and were, like many schools across the country, integrating this anniversary into their curriculum. Dance was no exception. I had long discussions with three Year

4 groups about what life was like for those at home and those at war in 1914 as the war was starting. We had been asked to make a dance for the Christmas performance based on 'that' football game when German and British soldiers came together in No Man's Land on Christmas Day to play football during a ceasefire. Discussions with the children progressed over a period of weeks, with them (and I) gaining a deep understanding and developing empathy with those young soldiers on both sides. The children were captivated, moved, and inspired, and took these discussions beyond the dance studio and into their homes. They talked with their families and brought back stories of great grandparents, eager to share with the group and to inform their movement. We made a moving piece of dance, expressing our research. The dance outcome had the desired effect of reducing their parents to tears! The creative process is, and was certainly in this case, one of collaboration and co-constructivism. We worked together, drawing on their work in class, and the making of the piece subsequently enriched their learning and understanding of this period in history.

Another curriculum area that can be supported effectively by dance is science. Topics that explore, for example, states of matter have many complex scientific concepts and unfamiliar words for children to learn, understand, and remember. When I explore these topics with children in a dance context, I always begin by asking the children what the properties of water are. There are compelling reasons for this. Water is a familiar substance and we can draw out children's understanding of the properties through discussion. Here, we would make a list and I would be looking for qualitative words such as: pourable, takes on the shape of its container, flows, etc. These are words that can translate to movement, and children can very quickly begin to truly understand their meaning through a dance idea. For example, we might play a game called 'fitting in'.

In pairs, 'A' makes a shape and holds it still. 'B' pours his or herself into that shape, thereby fitting in. A then steps away carefully and repeats the pouring in into B's shape. Often, children find themselves stuck on the floor and having nowhere else to move to. I would then introduce some dance vocabulary for them to explore how to 'get unstuck'. Children begin to learn about the three levels (high, middle and low) of dance. They will often choose not to use the low level, which means that they can keep the game going for longer, moving in a smooth, pourable way. This activity would take at least one lesson.

States of matter will include the concept of changing state, and in the classroom, children will learn what happens to water when it is heated and cooled. In dance, we would embed and consolidate their learning by playing with the question: 'what happens when…'

When water is boiled, the particles begin to **move** in an **excitable** way and some **escape** the surface of the water.

At this point, we might play the 'popcorn' game. Children take the numbers one to four. They all begin by crouching and then jump explosively straight up and back to crouching when their number is called. The caller gets faster, and the outcome is a class of children that resembles a pot of boiling, bubbling water - and with much laughter! This concept can be taken further into properties of gases and solids, and the language is all there in the science curriculum! For example, in a solid, particles are bound together by a stronger force than in liquid or gas. Expressing this concept through movement is very effective, and children can gain a greater understanding of how particles behave.

I feel that dance can and should be inclusive and accessible to all children and classroom teachers. The basic principles of a dance lesson allow for contextualisation, exploration, performance (sharing) and discussion. These are:

- Warming up;

- What are we learning?

- Set a short task;

- Watch and feedback;

- Warm down.

It is important to understand that the discussion stage involves peer and teacher feedback. This encourages analytical and critical language development of both dance and subject area. At this time when children and teachers are governed by deadlines and standardised testing, dance can offer opportunities to explore playfully and creatively, solving problems and accessing curriculum areas through embodied movement, adding value to the work of the school and unhindered by the need to provide 'evidence'. Dance is still on the curriculum, so why not use this timetabled space in the hall to support and explore children's learning? I am never surprised at the incredible performance outcomes that this approach produces, with work that has been created by the children. It is truly their own!

If you are reading this and are inspired to have a go...

- At the risk of contradicting myself, do not always look for a dance outcome. Children will perform each time they show you a small idea, and this should be celebrated.

- Use the time and space on your timetable to try it.

- Be playful, explore, create and do not be afraid to fail.

Chapter 7

The Birth of the Baby Lab

Guiako Obin

I have always been passionate about new technologies and how they positively impact on people's lives. In 2014, with some friends who share the same hobby, I took a massive online open course (MOOC) - about digital manufacturing offered by the reputed French school, *Institut Mines-Télécom*. During this course, we discovered a concept new to us – fablabs or manufacturing laboratories. The more we learned about this new kind of manufacturing workshops in western countries, the more this idea resonated with us in the African continent and particularly in the Ivorian context, where we live.

We believe that fablabs have a key role in spreading science to reinvent the habits of the people of the Ivorian territory. To adapt this western concept to the Ivorian context, our approach was centred around the philosophy of turning working-class neighbourhoods into innovation hubs to drive social transformation through digital means. We, therefore, chose to settle in Abobo, one of the poorest boroughs of the Ivory Coast, where we created the Baby Lab - the first Ivorian fablab.

The success of the Baby Lab is based on its positive social impact in the borough of Abobo, sadly famous for having the highest rate of crime and violence in the country, especially among young people who represent a great proportion of the unemployed. Our mission is to keep young people and children safe from youth crime, by helping them build careers in science and technology - fields where there are more employment opportunities which promote positive life outcomes. To make a small point on the town of Abobo in connection with the post-election crisis, I can add that this town has paid a heavy price in terms of victims, collateral damage, looting and repression. There was an 'invisible commando' where members fuelled armed conflict against the police over several weeks. There were losses of human life, including the killing of eight women during a march which has led to much debate in the press.

Displaced populations have been observed towards other towns and cities of the Ivory Coast. This military political crisis has weakened the municipality and had a negative impact on young people with rising figures of children in conflict with the law. The Party of Abobo is a notorious gang of young people who have committed crimes in the neighbourhoods of Abidjan since the day after the post-electoral crisis of April 2011. They are often armed with weapons and conduct random attacks.

Protected by former rebels (according to some sources), they engage as much in the trafficking of drugs as in the racket of the drivers of collective taxis (gbakas). The reaction of the authorities is slow, so instead, the inhabitants of the neighbourhoods organise to do justice themselves. Given this post-crisis state of affairs, we wanted to make a very positive change in Abobo. We did this by establishing the first laboratory of technological innovation to drive development and social transformation. It is interesting for us to see the impact of a project such as Baby Lab on individuals living in this community, given our focus on inclusive social development. We used my family house to start our laboratory which again strengthened our bonds with the community.

How we convinced people around us to support us in this project

We highlighted evidence of our social impact to all people and or organisations that can support us. The history of the municipal conflict in Abobo is well known, particularly the riots that took place during the post-electoral crisis. These events confirm the need for community strengthening initiatives on the territory. We started the Baby Lab with little financial support. Already having a place to launch it (my family home), we borrowed computers from our friends who work in companies and held spontaneous technology-based activities with the children from the neighbourhood. We worked like that for a year before receiving a visit from the former French Digital Secretary, Axelle Lemaire, who awarded us with our first grant through the French Embassy in the Ivory Coast. During an outreach mission to set up their innovation laboratory in Dakar to invent the bank of tomorrow, the Societe Generale Ivory Coast offered us ten computers when they decided to renew their stock. This contributed towards our first computer park.

Today, following national and international calls for projects that we have won, we have been able to receive grants and start cooperative programmes with the International Organisation of La Francophonie, the Digital Youth Foundation established by the Ministry of the Digital Economy and the Ivory Coast Post, the Orange Foundation, the Shared Foundation of the Webhelp Group, the Aldinie Foundation of the Maltem Consulting Group and UNICEF. I want to say a big thank you to these partners who continue to support us and with whom we want to build a common dream: to build digital communities of change across the continent.

The mission of Baby Lab

To develop the creativity and the innovator's spirit of young people from disadvantaged neighbourhoods, who often struggle to access basic resources for their development, Babylab gives young people the desire to believe in a better future for them and their community by using digital technology which, once its principles are under control, can help the development of local people. We call the young people working with us who have understood our commitment to the development of the territory by volunteering digital training citizen trainers. For example, our current fablab Manager Beucler Kpagni, after studying geography at university, initially committed to train several communities of children aged eight to 15 as part of our Kid Lab programme. He intervenes in schools and on specific missions in collaboration with other partners.

Baby Lab's educational 'maker' approach

Our training is provided by our network of trainers, who run workshops throughout the programmes. We have an active, collaborative and participative pedagogical approach. To do this, we rely on:

- Software platforms (scratch developed by MIT) and play kits specially designed for children (Makey Makey invention kits, robotics kits from Makeblock);

- Adapted thematic presentations (frugal innovation, social and solidarity economy, circular economy, open source and free software, science and technology);

- Group work reinforcing team spirit (collaborative projects);

- Tests to assess comprehension;

- Business project development; and

- Travelling awareness and training for geographically remote locations.

What I call citizenship in the digital world is giving a social and solidarity dimension to the technological development of the Ivorian territory by actively engaging populations to participate in activities.

The results

Since its creation in 2014, less than 5 years after its launch:

- More than 250 children from eight to 15 years old have been trained in computer coding, electronics and robotics, 36% of whom are girls.

- 86 digital workshops were delivered involving more than 4,000 participants.

- We have participated in 24 international meetings (Africa, Europe and North America).

- We have received 11 awards and recognitions.

- Baby Lab was a winner of three calls for projects from foundations of companies and international organisations.

- We have been featured in approximately twenty national and international newspapers, TV, and radio articles.

Areas for development

With each experience and project, we learned many things. We want to develop greater awareness of how to enable more young girls to become interested in science and technology.

- We want to add new training modules on other current topics (circular economy or the promotion of green jobs etc).

- A new opening means a new location and so the most important point is to adapt to the realities of the territory where the lab is developed.

The advice we would give to someone who wants to open a makerspace

In our opinion and based upon our experience, the creation of a makerspace must start from communities and not from the government. It needs to have an inclusive nature and be open to all to have great social impact. The makerspace must consider the realities of the ecosystem in which it wants to evolve. It must integrate and involve local people from the makerspace reflection phase to the monitoring and evaluation of the programmes developed for the target populations.

The well-being of individuals will have to be at the heart of the whole strategy and the access of girls and children to the various programmes should be prioritised. Labs are for us alternative schools that can strengthen or support the education systems of African countries. Students can come and practice fields of science in the margins of school curricula. Our local governments must see in these places of technological innovation opportunities for capacity building for the population and open more job opportunities.

Chapter 8

Starting a STEM Lab from Scratch

Andrey Guryev

I first became involved in teaching STEM in 2009, when it was suggested that I deliver robotics to pupils as an extracurricular subject after school. I was responsible for creating the programme of study for the pupils who were enrolled in the course. Parents are more likely to enrol their children in courses if they believe the programme of study is interesting and relevant. If the parents do not like the programme, then you will be left with no pupils. We must not forget, most importantly, the process of learning should be exciting and educational for the pupils, otherwise they will become bored and not attend the optional lessons.

During the first year of the STEM course delivery, so many pupils came to my lessons that I had to organise additional groups. Then I began to use STEM in my lessons, using different types of learning, primarily project based, where a variety of topics were related to real life. I had several ready-made project topics, but more often the children came up with what they would do.

For example, one night much snow fell before a lesson and it was complicated to walk outside - everything was covered in snow - and the pupils decided to make the 'the snow-moving car' project. During the process of creation, they learned more about the problem from a scientific point of view, obtaining information from the teacher and the internet. Afterwards, they were able to draw on paper how their snow-moving car would look like, they considered its mathematical and technical sides, and later they created the model using a construction set and other materials of choice (cardboard, coloured paper, glue etc) so that in the end, everyone had their own unique model.

When the model was ready, everyone presented theirs and demonstrated how it worked. For the three remaining minutes of each presentation, the children and facilitators carried out an overall evaluation, what were the advantages and disadvantages of the design of each model, and how the design could be improved. The lesson was divided into 90 minutes with a ten-minute rest break. Some projects were completed in two to three sessions.

The children really enjoyed this approach. They solved many tasks independently in a competition-like format. The role of the teacher was as a mentor, to help the students and guide them. The children understood the learning process of the project's activities. They identified and appreciated how one project could be associated with a variety of disciplines.

The lessons can be delivered so that pupils work individually, where each pupil can make their own creative task on an overall theme and every student gets to complete their own given project. There are also collaborative projects, where every child or group contributes towards part of an overall project, which can be combined to create one main project at a later stage.

I tried to deliver cross-curricular STEM content in school during a technology lesson, but it was more complicated to do, as each lesson was divided into 45 minutes. We overcame this challenge in the following way: in the first 45-minute lesson, we thought through the project and planned the design of the product, and the following lesson involved practical work where the design was created.

I used the same learning framework in the children's technology park 'Quantorium' where the pupils work on practical cases. The governmental educational organisations can have many bureaucratic restrictions, which do not allow for the full application of STEM subjects. For this reason, I organised my laboratory for robotics and high technology as the ASLab - where we can fully study STEM subjects without bureaucracy.

In our lab, pupils are grouped in various ways. The level of the pupil can be assessed at the beginning of the school year, in one group there can be children from different age groups, but a similar level of physical construction and programming experience. We can also group according to age where appropriate. The youngest group caters to pupils from five to seven years, the middle group is for pupils from seven to nine years, the senior group is for those who are ten to 12 years, and the advanced group is for students from 13 to 16 years. The youngest and middle groups mostly study through learning the basic principles of construction and programming and various entry-level technologies.

The advanced group, who have already mastered the basics, continue to study more higher technology, such as 3D printing, the laser cutting of materials, electronics and soldering, working with diverse equipment, programming, internet of things and designing more complex work. They work more often in groups of two or three. Their ideal project of choice is often taken from a real-life problem or they find an idea on the internet, which they later develop during practical work in the lab.

Unlike younger groups, senior and advanced groups are constantly engaged through online resources. These groups have common chats in which they frequently communicate and remotely solve some tasks related to the projects. Also, children conduct classes themselves under the status of a teacher - they are given a topic that they themselves study or that they are interested in, they then prepare a lesson and share knowledge about this topic with the rest of the group.

Pupils who study for many years at the lab, starting from 14 (the minimum working age for children in Russia) can officially work in the laboratory and become a full-fledged employee at a rate of 0.25. In their free time from mainstream study, they can make a practical project in the laboratory and obtain wages for it.

For pupils from 16 years and older, we organised the module 'business and entrepreneurship', in which pupils learn the basics of entrepreneurship. In the process of the lesson taking place in a given course, the pupils create their project. The project is then shared at a start-up with one of our laboratory partners or they could independently bring it to the market under the status of 'an individual entrepreneur', which can be issued at the age of 18. In this way, our lab organises a full cycle of lessons with children beginning from five years (the very basic principles of physical construction and programming) to 18 years when young people can commercially collaborate or launch their own business. We have also introduced a new financial literacy and investment module for young people.

Quite recently, we decided to share our experiences with all those who are interested in STEM education and created a channel on youtube,[12] on which I and students soon will cover a variety of STEM activities and competitions, talk about various equipment, methods and lifehacks. Soon we will release a cycle of video clips about how to organise your own STEM lab from scratch.

We will share and show how we study in the ASLab so that everyone can try and adapt our activities wherever they are in the world.

Chapter 9

Tracing the Development of the 'Innovation Master Class with Lego Mindstorms EV3' for Warwick Manufacturing Group (WMG) at the University of Warwick

Dr Ali J. Ahmad

Warwick Manufacturing Group (WMG) at the University of Warwick is a globally renowned centre of excellence in academia-industry collaboration. WMG's research outputs, which are mostly technology and engineering-orientated, aim to make a direct impact on the commercial performance of its industrial partners. The outputs of WMG's research inform the design, content, and pedagogic approaches of its 15 different postgraduate and several undergraduate programmes. A vocational ethos drives the teaching and learning environment at WMG; teaching members of staff come from a wide variety of industry and academic backgrounds and aim to impart education where the aim is to be 'hands-on' for creating new 'makers'. I teach postgraduate students, who are undertaking a variety of MSc qualifications the subject 'innovation'. Innovation is taught in a module, comprising approximately 40 contact hours, spread over a week in the 0900-1830 format. This format allows for an extended amount of 'facetime' with students and enables me to design sessions around specific topics linked to the module's learning outcomes. The sessions, each 1-1/2 hour and five per day, can be merged to create teaching and learning workshops.

When I took over the innovation module in 2013, WMG gave me 'artistic freedom' to completely redesign its pedagogic method – to bring it in-line with the latest thinking in the area and to infuse it with a vocational ethos. Instructor-led content was put in place, a new day-long 'disruptive innovation' workshop based on the Nintendo Wii was designed, and an online simulation to teach innovation management was sourced from a vendor. What I wanted was something far ahead of its time as a final send-off learning experience for my students. After all, the module was titled innovation - there were high expectations for WMG.

While studying the online content allied to an innovation textbook, I came across a session based on LEGO Mindstorms NXT proposed by respected UK academics Goffin and Mitchell – based at Cranfield University. I was immediately drawn to the prospect of using programmable LEGO, with all its versatility, to design a day-long workshop to give my students a unique learning experience – one which they would not experience in any other WMG module. I researched LEGO Mindstorms NXT and contacted LEGO Education UK who put me in touch with a certified trainer. That initial conversation with the trainer on the phone helped me understand the potential and limits of Mindstorms when considering the confines of WMG's pedagogic scope and the background of my students (primarily from overseas developing and emerging economies).

I also had to consider my ability to facilitate a high impact learning experience for 35 students in an instance of the innovation module. The module is delivered approximately eight times per academic year for the UK full-time students (21 to 22-year olds), twice for our industry participants (experienced executives), and overseas at our partner institutions in Hong Kong, Singapore, Thailand, Turkey and Malaysia. I asked myself: will I be able to deliver the Mindstorms-based workshop effectively each time in a variety of different locations with varied participant profiles? I did not have a clear answer to this question but was up to the challenge. Hence, I created a 'planned investment estimate' for the consideration of the director of WMG's Education Programmes, who I had to subsequently bring on board for budgetary approval. The director posed valid questions, such as: is any prior learning needed for the students? How will you assess the students' performance? What are the key learning outcomes for this new session? Are there limits to the total number of students per team? What is unique about Mindstorms and how is it superior to other potentially competing platforms? Are these kits durable? and, so on. These probing questions helped me think about practicalities and impact, while remaining focussed on my principle aim: showcasing the innovation module with educational innovations.

As a result, I was able to acquire 6 LEGO Mindstorms (Basic) NXT sets along with a day-long training session from a LEGO education trainer. I only had the rough skeletal structure of the day-long workshop in my mind at this point-in-time; but I knew that after my own practical hands-on experience with Mindstorms – both the kit and the NXT programming environment – I would be able to conjure up enough details to plan and execute the envisaged workshop. I titled it 'AutoConvoy Challenge with LEGO Mindstorms NXT' and began to play out how the day would unfold for a typical student.

I tried this approach due to several important pedagogical reasons: first, getting students' buy-in – this was for me essential, because I believe no learning is possible without the active participation of the learner in their own learning. How would I get this buy-in? Thinking from the students' perspective – after having gone through four already very long and intense days – if I were a student then I'd be looking forward to the end of the module arriving sooner rather than later. To get a tired and weary student's buy-in for a final day-long workshop would require something exceptional and never experienced.

Second, I knew that whatever I was going to put forth ought to have something to do with play. We have done the work these past four days – it is now time to put what we have learnt into practice through the medium of play. The importance of play is acknowledged and widely approved in the innovation literature and students are exposed to the notion that if one were to study the history of the development of most new innovations - whether scientific, technological or business – one would find that the subject innovator stumbled onto something new by chance or created something new while tinkering or simply messing around. I wanted to allow my students to deploy their creative energies, work together collaboratively, and solve a serious commercial / industrial problem by disguising the learning experience as non-serious.

Third, in the module – during the previous four days, students would be exposed to concepts such as trial and error, effectuation, creative thinking, understanding and breaking down problems; topics that are linked to learning 'about' innovation. I wanted to design a workshop that would enable learning 'for' *doing* innovation – which is entirely different. Bridging the for and about gap was essential for closing the learning loop. It is one thing to read about, listen to, and discuss risk, uncertainty, project management, budgetary controls, and opportunity evaluation – but an entirely different thing when actually feeling the pressure that comes from taking personal risks or taking risks on behalf of a team whose members are relying on you to get things right, effectuate solutions to problems as they arise in real time, and so on. The workshop under design was going to give students a chance to see and feel the challenges and pleasures of doing innovation in a controlled and fun way – a physical simulation.

Finally, I wanted to create a memorable and eventful experience for students that would raise the profile of the Innovation module and generate positive student feedback. I know that learning retention is a problem; most students, after about a week post a module, have retained, at the most, between 5-8% of the content. The rest of the content usually fails to influence thinking or to create future recall to influence managerial or entrepreneurial behaviour. Amongst other factors, the problem of retention has to do with the human attention span, which starts to taper off after 15 minutes of System 2-type (rational) intensive learning. After about a year, I would be surprised if they even remember the module tutor's name. What if I could design an immersive and fun learning experience, the outcomes of which could be easily recalled even after multiple years had gone by. I looked back into my own educational history and thought to myself; from which experiences at university did I recall the most? Which experiences cast a lasting impression and made me think later in professional life when I was taking real-world professional decisions? My mind recalled those sessions best where I created something new and different when working with others (both due to pleasure and trauma) – a piece of software for my MSc, an ethnographic report for my MPhil and a poster for my PhD. The workshop under design had the right ingredients – students would work together in a group to tackle a (commercial / industrial) problem through the medium of play to create something physical and original – new to the world. They would not forget their LEGO creations and the solutions such creations had the potential to provide (if built) to industrial partners.

I created a Moodle[13] mini-site to walk the students through the day. The day commenced with a 15-minute presentation by me on 'autonomous vehicles'. This presentation was meant to pump-prime the students on the potentials of robotics and AI as applied to the domain of personal and public land transport. After the presentation, the workshop's background was explained as follows:

An automobile company (like Jaguar Land Rover or Toyota) with a diverse range of vehicles pitched at different market segments is finding that it is slipping into the typical trough of slow growth and low returns from its existing range. The management believes that a new market opportunity exists in the goods transport sector: road convoys - where a fleet of vehicles travelling over long distances can follow a lead vehicle, braking and accelerating, thereby travelling as a convoy. To prove this concept, the management has assembled five multidisciplinary teams within the organisation. *You* are part of a team invited to pitch your proof-of-concept along with its business case to the management.

I then proceeded to explain that each team (which I created prior based on my assessment of students' personalities during the previous four days of interaction), in competition with others was going to have to demonstrate two outcomes (as under). I also introduced an element of cooperation – because a convoy is based on multiple vehicles and each team had to collaborate towards the end to ensure that the convoy worked – one team's output's failure had the potential to jeopardise the entire convoy.

Therefore, working co-opetively (competitive and collaborative), each team needed to demonstrate that:

1. Their 'proof-of-concept' works; demonstrating the same independently and as a part of a convoy.

2. They have a strong commercial case backed by real world market research on a customer (how will that particular customer save money or generate a new income from 'your' innovation?).

Teams were cautioned: 'management' requires that the following be adhered to:

1. The investment in the project is capped at £500.

2. The deadlines must be met as per schedule, no extra time will be given under any circumstances.

3. The team presentation must last ten minutes.

Each team had typically six to seven members and were advised to choose a team leader. They were assigned a working space – a separate syndicate room and a desktop with the NXT programming environment pre-installed. Within the team, students were to take on one of the following functional roles:

1. Commercial research and case development;

2. Finance;

3. Physical design and assembly;

4. Software design and testing;

5. Manufacturing; and

6. General management.

Teams were required to develop a budget and keep track of their expenditures in the following areas:

1. Technical advice - @ £10 per-minute.

2. Business consultancy - @ £10 per-minute.

3. Parts and materials - @ £1 per-component (LEGO piece).

4. Manufacturing - @ £1 per-minute of factory time (at actuals).

5. Programming - @ £1 per-minute.

6. Testing - @ £5 per-minute.

Presentation requirements were provided along with the workflow and deadlines as per the following scheme:

1. Attending a de-briefing by their organisation's Board of Directors (BoD).

2. Pitching an initial design concept, along with its commercial potential to the management. The management at this stage will monitor the project's budget, parts sourcing, manufacturing, assembly and testing strategies. The team must secure BoD buy-in and approval at this stage.

3. Producing product and presentation.

4. Testing the prototype.

5. Demonstrating the prototype.

6. Presenting the new product concept to the management.

Students were required to manage their own time – they were free to take breaks for tea and lunch whenever they wished – keeping in view their own task completion timelines. I also knew students would ask questions about the assessment. I made the entire criteria and my assessment template downloadable via Moodle. Assessment was undertaken at three stages – once at point 2 above (at 1230), and then points 5 (1530) and 6 (1630). The weightage was 20% to the output and 80% to the process with criteria to judge performance on various parameters linked to effective innovation management.

Observations and results

The first instance of the AutoInnovation Challenge was audited by a professor and a senior research fellow. These were colleagues I had requested to be available on the day to help me troubleshoot and to take note of aspects where improvements could be introduced in future instances. I also enlisted the help of a PhD student with a background in artificial intelligence.

I started taking mental notes right from the moment when I brought the new Mindstorms NXT kits into the lecture room – the students were visibly impressed and came to look and asked questions – which were encouraging signs. The workshop commenced at 0900 with the presentation on autonomous vehicles which made use of interesting YouTube clips of autonomous features in existing cars and trucks – such as self-parking, lane assist, and even self-driving (Google Car). The energy in the room was heightened as I asked students to think about the problems that fossil fuel-based cars driven by humans create (environmental damage, increasing commuting times, accidents, congestion on roads and so on). Student participation was satisfactory because they were able to relate to these known problems. By 0920 I had begun the explanation of how the day would proceed and gave comprehensive guidelines on what was required. I did see confused and worried faces towards the end when I presented a quick overview of the NXT kits. To ease students' subconscious concerns – I reassured them by saying "do not worry, the kits are designed for children eight and above – if they can cope, so can you" – this statement was guaranteed to elicit smiles. I also told them that learning in this task would be primarily self-directed – via the do it yourself and learn it yourself – way with me only pointing them in the right direction at critical junctures.

Students did not raise any concerns about their team allocations – although I did offer to change any student's team should they need me to. When the teams were settled in their respective syndicate rooms, I started to do my rounds from 1000 along with my assistant. The auditors too dropped in and out keeping a tab on how the day was progressing. Some teams were clearly anxious, others were keen and still others appeared to lack energy. I spent about 15 minutes with each team to help them 'get started' by (a) moderating the appointment of a team leader and distributing roles and responsibilities, (b) explaining how to think about the 'problem' in a structured way by asking 'why' type questions, and (c) helping them look up NXT vehicle designs online and watching YouTube videos of other makers to draw inspiration for their own product (they were not allowed to use the Mindstorms manual). By 1045, all teams had started to make progress, some though were getting too bogged down in detail and had lost sight of their timelines. By making another set of rounds at 1100 I reminded the teams that they must start building with a design in place by maximum 1115 to be ready with a basic prototype for the 1230 first round assessment. This warning was enough to get teams into 'play' mode – which was admittedly messy because too many team members were trying to get involved at the same time.

When I began my first round of assessment, most teams had built a basic vehicle – some were three-wheeled while others were four-wheeled. No team though had an answer to the question "how much money have you spent thus far?" This came as a wake-up call to them because in their excitement to create, they had lost sight of 'managerial control'. I warned them that the company BoD expects to know their expense figure to-date; and that poor financial management would reflect negatively on the team's over-all performance. They were warned that If they could not effectively manage a mere £500, then how could they be trusted to manage £5,000 or £50,000 in further iterations of their prototype. Soon after, students were encouraged to take a lunch break – some teams decided not to (and order food in instead) because they were having 'too much fun' and 'had a lot to do'

By approximately 1330, product testing had begun which is where another level of complexity arose – the NXT programming environment. To facilitate, I asked all the teams' programmers to attend in the main lecture room a tutorial. My assistant ran the 30-minute tutorial, giving them enough detail on how to access help files and to create basic move-stop and follow-a-line programmes. Hints were given on how to create a 'convoying' programme (which required the use of both the ultrasonic and light sensors). Students seemed reasonably satisfied and were eager to return to their teams to begin the programming task. While this tutorial was going on, I held another side session with the 'commercial case developers' – took note of their concerns, helped them think through their business cases and pointed them in the right direction when it came to collating and presenting market research data. I reminded them that their role was fundamental to the team's overall success, in that what good is a new product if there is no market for it?

A test track was created in the main lecture room by connecting several flat-surfaced tables and electrical insulation tape. Each time a team wanted to test their robot, they had to make their way to the test track. I could sense that this was causing students some frustration (because of the time wasted walking back and forth from the syndicates to the main lecture room). I thought to myself that trial and error is meant to be frustrating. When the pressure was too intense at around 1500, I did put a line of electrical insulation tape down in their syndicate rooms to help the teams run successive trials much quicker.

Each team was aiming to create a vehicle that would do three laps of the test track with the fastest time and least amount of errors (such as going off track). The design of the track itself presented challenges to the teams, some of the corners were somewhat sharp (although rounded) and vehicles based on a 4-wheeled design had too wide a turning circle which meant that it was impossible for them to successfully complete a lap. Necessarily, the teams had to quickly improvise changes to their hardware. With time running short, and design changes and programming occurring simultaneously – I could sense the pressure and frustration that some members of teams were feeling. At 1530, out of five teams – only two had reasonably well designed and working vehicles. I asked all teams to stop working immediately and to join me in the main lecture room. There was a lot of groaning and muttering under the breath; I knew they wanted more time to try and 'get it right'. I told them that they had invested nearly a full day in the design and build task, and that they were doing exceedingly well. I encouraged them to remain focussed and to not get anxious and that I was giving them an extra 30 minutes. With my assistant and I troubleshooting for the teams (while advising them to keep all records of money spent on the two forms of consultancy), we got them ready to demonstrate in the race and convoy challenges for 1600.

The challenges were very well received. Before the demonstrations began, I thanked all the students for their participation and for making the day a success. Lots of videos were made and photos were taken, background music scores were also played to energise the demonstration – all interspersed with rounds of applause and laughter. The presentations began at 1700 – approximately 45 minutes late, each lasting between eight to ten minutes followed by probing questions by me. I consciously mimicked the style often seen and heard on the BBC TV show Dragon's Den to simulate a real-world dialogue. The day ended with the teams being asked to disassemble their creations and to organise their kits for future use.

Moving forward

Since 2013, the *AutoInnovation challenge* has gone through two major updates – it is now based on the EV3 platform and has been re-titled 'innovation masterclass with Lego Mindstorms EV3'. Many minor refinements have been made over the years to streamline the overall learning experience. These have been based on student feedback, peer observations, and my own reflections. Simple refinements such as advising students to pre-install the NXT/EV3 software on their laptops a day before, providing a budgeted vs actual template, a Gantt Chart format with critical deadlines plotted, ensuring batteries are charged prior and double-checking whether the disassembled materials are kept back as per the kit boxes' formats have allowed students to take back more from the workshop in terms of new learning.

One thing that did cause serious problems was the shipping of the kits to WMG's overseas centres. The kits got stopped at customs, duties had to be paid, and when they finally arrived, we found them opened and rummaged through. It took countless hours reconciling them and double checking whether all components were in place for students to use. Since then, WMG's partners have invested in their own kits. I also found that if students were given a carte blanche to think up any product to solve a hypothetical problem for any industry, problems arose. Ideation took too long and was quite unstructured, the build-off became overly complicated, and the level of programming expertise needed to make the product work could not be developed in a matter of a few hours – especially since most students had no prior experience with coding.

The first version of the workshop was focused on a very specific product and industry – which made the process and outputs regimented and confined, respectively. The second version was too broad to make the process too unpredictable and risky and the output incomplete and invaluable. The current EV3-based version is based on the 'anthropic principle' and is about staying in 'goldilocks' or 'just right' zones when it came to delivering an impactful and memorable learning experience. Using EV3, students design, build and create commercial cases for new products based on AI and robotics that a consumer electronics company could launch to solve problems for existing businesses. By giving students examples of what previous teams had developed, I am able to provide a reasonable level of confidence to students right from the on-set that the task ahead for them is achievable and that they are not purposefully set up to fail.

To those wishing to replicate my work, whether at a university, college or even school – I can offer the following tips:

1. Think carefully about how the Mindstorms-based session links into your course's / programme's overall pedagogical philosophy. More specifically, how it delivers on the set learning outcomes you have developed and how learning from it would be assessed and fed back to students.

2. The availability of facilities is essential along with pre-planning. Adequately equipped and private working spaces, laptops with the software installed (some students inevitably forget to bring theirs or with NXT it cannot be installed on MAC OS), batteries ought to be pre-charged, and the kits audited. The last thing we want as management educators is being accused of mismanagement.

3. Have suitable help available – servicing five to six teams of six to seven students each is challenging for a single tutor due to the breadth and scale of the workshop. At least two tutors are recommended.

4. A thoughtful allocation of students to teams is important. I did not have a lot of confidence in teaming-up tools; I rely on my own judgement and pinpoint individuals who could potentially lead teams prior. I attempt to make the distribution of students across teams equitable with a good mix of genders, nationalities and personalities (without potential clashes) represented.

5. Make yourself available and visible to students throughout the day so that they have the confidence that they are being looked after. Positively intervene if you believe that some teams might be veering into the wrong direction with either the build task or the commercial case development. Advise them of potential hazards, unanswered questions they should be considering and convince them to re-evaluate their approach if you know they would lose marks at any assessment stage.

6. Students are ultimately output focused – they did not care much about the process (which they might reflect on later). It is worthwhile to ensure that all teams have something to demonstrate at the end of

the day and that their presentation is of an acceptable standard. If this requires bending the rules a little bit, then as a tutor you should consider the merits of doing so. A team with nothing to show for at the end of the day with a lot of work put in, is deflated and demotivated. Do explain to them, however, if you do decide to bend the rules and create their programme for them, for example, that not all ideas become innovations. Nearly eight out of ten fail; but failure is important in innovation because it is through failure that one learns which mistakes to avoid in the next attempt.

7. Finally, enjoy yourself with the students – be harsh and critical when needed, especially during assessment stages to simulate real world stresses but also be a coach and mentor – creating an environment where they could motivate themselves and move forward, not accept defeat. Show students that you are there to help and that their learning is your top priority. Appreciate everyone in the end and be generous in your marking!

Learning technologies like the EV3 platform are only useful as pedagogic tools when the tutors who deploy them are forward thinkers and reflective. It is important to consider the return on investment – the kits are expensive, think about how frequently you will use them and for how long. Can you perhaps use something less complicated and cheaper like Meccano or Scalextric? If not integrated properly into the curriculum, EV3-type learning technologies can produce blow-back which might ultimately lead to negative student feedback.

Chapter 10

Project-Based Learning: A Transdisciplinary Learning Experience

Mala Sinha

Science is as much about satiating our curiosity and sense of wonderment as it is about solving human and environmental problems. Problem solving demands increasing collaboration across all boundaries we have constructed either socially or politically, simply because most problems are of global magnitude. In a fast-changing world of higher complexity, the context of education is also fast evolving and demands more dynamic teaching and learning approaches. We need to constantly re-align these to match the demands of society. The struggle for the educators of today is to bring relevance to the classroom in a world where content is available online and there is an information and knowledge overload. One effective way of doing this is through project-based learning (PBL).[14] PBL not only brings problem-solving to the forefront of learning, it also provides an opportunity for social learning. It is a powerful tool in an educator's repertoire. It repositions the learner into an active, independent student-centred space and the teachers into the role of a facilitator who provides an enriched and safe learning environment from the side-lines, supporting and buttressing student learning.

I am an International Baccalaureate (IB) diploma programme teacher. I have taught IB biology for three years and am gearing up to teach environment systems and societies next year. The IB curriculum does include student-led projects to develop the 21st century skills of students. Environment systems and societies (ESS) particularly lends itself extremely well to PBL. Students not only find it easy to observe and relate to many environmental issues around them, but they also can become actively involved in exploring the possibility of novel solutions.

The IB diploma programme is a two-year college preparatory, senior secondary level programme. The curriculum entails three mandatory PBL experiences. One is a collaborative science project involving all the science subjects viz physics, chemistry, biology, design technology, information technology, and ESS offered at the schools. The other two are more involved. They include an individual exploration and research and experimentation-based work. Both culminate in writing research papers, one in a nearly 1200 words lab report and the other in a 4000-word long research paper called the extended essay. The extended essay can be done in any content area of the student's choice while the lab reports have to be done for all the science subjects one is studying.

While the science project is confined to a pre-decided umbrella topic, the lab report and extended essay could be written on a subject and topic of the individual student's choice. While the science project requires group work, writing the lab report and extended essay are very personal journeys for the students.

I wish to share my experiences, and what I learnt from them as a novice, with all teachers. I will first share my experience with the trans-disciplinary science project in which students do have the choice to decide what problem from the umbrella topic on which they would like to work collaboratively.

Planning the entire project collaboratively and implementing it successfully is a fairly challenging job. Good planning by the teachers makes the journey for the learner easier and productive. The rubric for learning objectives and assessment is provided by the IB, we just had to design for the students' engagement. It is a good idea to have a rubric ready that aligns to the standards you are teaching. I did not have much prior experience of doing it either as a teacher or even as a student when we went to school and college. Project-based learning is something I learnt about only when I did my coursework for the teaching credentials. I did not implement it myself in my class during my pre-service teaching. My and my colleagues' educational experiences have been in very teacher-centred traditional classrooms. I noticed that all the science teachers involved in the project had a different understanding of this new kind of learning and assessment experience which was not enough to implement PBL lessons well. Our own learning experiences so far became our prior knowledge base. They not only can limit our understanding of something but also predispose the teacher to fall back upon what is most familiar to them when they find themselves caught in unfamiliar territory. The first year I focused too much on designing the individual labs, because it was the skill I knew how to teach well, while losing sight of the larger picture.

Having a clear understanding of the learning objectives set for the project along with well aligned assessment rubrics can help get over this problem. They worked for me. It gave focus as well as a road map for us to follow. In PBL, problem-solving is the most important aspect. We develop skills and content knowledge around identifying and solving that problem.

The topic of research: The umbrella topic we had for our students in the first year was 'The playfield'. This provided a wide choice for the students to pick any aspect of it right from the playfield itself, sports, sport-industry, athletes, sports equipment, technology in sports etc. Sports will not be the same without the spectators, so that was also included in the list of aspects that could be studied. We chose this topic because sports generate interest easily and are something students take to readily. Most students follow sports news and would be aware of the latest news and issues. Generating interest and personal involvement is very important to sustain students' interest and keeping them engaged through the protracted project. Otherwise, they see it as just another task and do it perfunctorily. In the second year, the topic given to them was 'beverages'.

Prepping the students: My struggle as a 'novice' teacher was to introduce the topic and get the students to identify and agree upon a real-world problem to work on. Just declaring the topic and expecting the students to be able to figure things out does not work. There was a challenge here as many of my students, who had switched to IB from other curriculum schools which use traditional pedagogy, were used to only taking instructions and doing as instructed, not charting their own path. They can be at a complete loss when asked to think of what they could do on a given topic. In the first year, I shared the rubric with the students but did not discuss the thought behind the collaborative aspect or the problem-solving aspect of it well enough as I was not clear myself how to go about it. As a result, I had some well-written labs which were individually great but together they did not answer any problem.

Students need clarity on what they are expected to do and, more importantly, why. Once this is well-conveyed to the students, things start falling into place and the entire exercise becomes purposeful to the students. This does not mean that lessons need to be entirely teacher-led. After the chaotic experience of my first year, I fixed this problem the following year by explaining the purpose of the science project in the introductory session. For this, I briefly narrated the story of how people living in the suburbs around San Francisco Bay reported health issues.[15] The pattern was observed by a doctor, which sparked a study and resulted in the student-led activity of solving a significant human and environmental problem in that area. I asked my students to imagine if they were that doctor who observed this pattern and wanted to examine the issue:

1. What could be the possible reasons for the health issues, hence, subject areas they would like to study to analyse the problem?

2. Would they be able to study it all alone?

3. Who (field experts) would they want on their team to research the issue?

4. What would their approach be to identify and solve the problem?

By answering these questions, not only did the students list the possible reasons they also realised that different field experts were needed on the team to work collaboratively to understand the inter-laced complexity in the natural world. In addition, they realised how observations in the real-world lead to asking questions and kickstarting the scientific method of experimentation to find explanations and solutions to problems. The students took the role of not just a problem-solving team of scientists but one of problem identifiers too. This time students had far more clarity on framing problem statements for their groups as well as designing meaningful labs. Their individual experiments were more relevant to the problem and more purposeful.

This is also where an important key element of PBL plays out, which makes the students independent learners. They need to be inducted into a routine of thinking, discussing, generating their own plans, and taking ownership of their learning and their work. Having thinking routines scaffolded by 'sentence stems' and 'thinking prompts' recording their feelings, reasoning, and reactions can be an extremely important metacognitive practice at this point. For example – "I feel strongly about... because..., therefore, we need to find..." or "I feel the problem of... in competitive sports is ...because..., therefore, I need to find...". Discussions guided around these give a direction to their thinking in framing good problem statements.

Everybody learns: Like in all group situations, some self-motivated, competitive or aggressive students may sometimes do all the work while the shy, less assertive or less motivated students may lose interest. A safe learning environment needs to be created where everybody gets to speak their mind, gets to contribute, be of value to the team and take pride in what they have done and learnt. Assigning roles in a group helps giving the routine a structure: like the roles of a facilitator, recorder, timekeeper, presenter etc so that everyone is engaged.

Alternatively, you can have assorted groups in the cohort. Students in each group can study an aspect of the problem through a different lens - biology, physics or chemistry. Computer science students can design data collection or data analysis tools. Design Technology students can help design special apparatus or gadgets. All students get to individually design their experiments related to the problem.

Guiding the students to plan their research: The sharper the research problem definition, the better the problem-solving and the greater the autonomy in thinking and doing for students. The challenge is really in defining the problem well. A challenge for the teacher is to keep steering the students towards the problem and not let them stray away from content as well as the problem. The experiment should be relevant to and contribute towards examining and helping solve the problem.

Debugging as we go: The first year left a lot to be desired. Students did design their labs and implemented them. They did collect data, analysed it but all the weaknesses came to the fore when they collated their results and made their presentations. Their work was disjointed, and no solutions could be proposed. Their labs, though individually good ones, were not necessarily relevant to the topic they had chosen. The problem itself was not well identified. In the second year this problem was addressed in the brief when the group project was introduced and the rubric was unpacked. Students' understanding of purpose, their role and expectations were made clearer this time. They identified and defined problems more clearly and consequently got closer to proposing solutions based on their findings. Their presentations were more coherent, and the students were more confident in presenting their findings simply because they made more sense now. The students had a sense of achievement that they were doing something useful. One group of students compared the sugar content in various carbonated drinks and compared it with homemade lemonade and presented to the students which drink they found was healthier and why. Another group designed a mechanical arm to pour coffee and sugar into a coffee maker. It was a good attempt at designing and assembling a gadget by the design technology students. In just one year we went from not having a product at all to some good quality coherent presentations to the school community. Next year when I introduce the PBL to my students, I will use a story where a tangible attention-grabbing product, which proves to be a change agent, has been presented to the community.

PBL provides much deeper and authentic student engagement as they produce original work of which they can take complete ownership of and take pride in.

Project-based experiences make learning wholesome, meaningful and make classrooms relevant. Doing this project, the students got to put themselves in the shoes of the scientists and look at the nature of science from that vantage point. It goes a long way in appreciating what science is about and how it works. They also learnt how important it is to work collaboratively to solve human and environmental problems.

The community engagement aspect of it has still not been met in the past two years. I hope to be able to get my students to come up with a quality product this year that can be shared with the community. That really is the benchmark of the success of the PBL. Hopefully this year we'll be able to get everything right. It takes a few years to learn and perfect it!

Each time you do it you would know what went wrong and you keep debugging your code to arrive at a better version than last time. You might want to sit down with your colleagues several times during the project implementation and reflect on how effectively the learning objectives are being met. Referring to a rubric frequently helps the teachers new to this in giving them confidence and do course corrections where needed. Review what worked, what did not work, how to fix what's not working. In the end it is an immensely gratifying effort.

PBL for writing the research paper: The second project-based experience is the extended essay. This is a much deeper, personal and protracted engagement culminating in an authentic academic paper the student must write based on the research they have conducted using either primary or secondary data from a reliable database. The student works individually and independently over a period of six to nine months to complete this task. They have the support from a chosen supervisor who provides guidance and measured feedback to the student through the process. The emphasis is more on walking through the process to refine skills like research-designing and communicating the findings using the academic language and protocol. Other 21st-century skills like critical thinking, social skills, and self-management skills are fostered through this engagement.

For the data collection, the students could either collect their own data or use secondary data sources. Before the students undertake this task, some skills are already in place. Students have done some labs and have learnt to hypothesise, identify variables, manipulate them using some lab techniques, used data loggers too, analysed the data, graphed it, and drawn conclusions from it. Since it is an assessed piece, it must be done with some prior preparation.

In the two years that I supervised a few students there were a few challenges that I, and just about every other teacher, faced. Getting started is often the most challenging phase. Firstly, most of them feel lost about what to write the essay about. To solve this, I am planning to have them compile a personal repository of their own questions that keep coming up in the class discussions. Students often ask questions in the class which are worth developing into an investigation. I am planning to have the students keep recording them somewhere - in their folders, section of notebook or a blank sheet posted on the display board at the back of the class - to draw research questions from later. We will code them as 'flagged questions'. I could explain to them in the beginning of the session itself why we are collecting these questions.

The next challenge they face is staying focused on the topic they choose. They, oftentimes, start with, let's say, try to prove that 'my fingers have three joints each' and finish with establishing 'my fingers are longer than my thumb'. They tend to drown in the enormity of the task and lose focus of what they want to say when writing such a long piece. This can largely be avoided by investing time and effort in writing a well-focused, clearly worded and lucid research question as well as hypotheses. Identifying and refining a good research question itself goes a long way in decluttering ideas in the students' minds. The road map for the rest becomes that much easier to lay out. While writing if they are frequently made to revisit the research question, their thoughts will stay on track and they will produce better work. To help them with this, I have identified and created a playlist of videos from various universities' research and writing labs. These are videos clips or activities on organising ideas, formulating the research questions, identifying variables, etc. You could curate your own playlist and customise for each student depending on what their areas for development are and where help is needed.

Another good and useful practice is to share the rubric as well as a couple of very good samples of marked extended essays from previous years with them. It gives them an idea of what the expectations are from them. Also, it is a good idea to choose two or three very different kinds of essays before sharing with the class. The problem with sharing only one sample is that it becomes the template and one naturally becomes disposed towards replicating it. The sample should not restrain their creativity.

A third challenge comes when they must write the conclusion. Evaluation is a higher order thinking skill. It does not come naturally to all the students. Even the best of them need support to develop this skill because it comes only from doing, at least a few times. Have the students analyse the data, try and establish correlation based on graphical tools and evaluate the study. For this, data from some studies could be used. They will also design and implement their own labs then evaluate them.

An important takeaway from this experience is that students learn the value of academic honesty and critical analysis of academic literature which they will have to study or generate when they go to university. This also develops critical literacy skills that all students need to be equipped with to be able to navigate through the deluge of information being generated and available to them, much of it coming from dubious sources and of questionable veracity.

Both these PBL experiences make one a lifelong learner. They not only equip students with enduring and timeless skills for learning but also the confidence to act in the face of a problem. Regardless of whether they go into academia or not, these skills do make for a literate society of citizens who will be able to appreciate the enormity of the problems faced by us as also prepare them to be able to make informed choices leading to sustainable development.

Chapter 11

Make Your School: A Creative Tech Workshop

Elena Tibi

Our society has changed rapidly from analogue to digital in the past two to three decades. Not only has digitalisation reformed the way we work, it has given birth to a new generation of young people: the digital natives, who grow up using digital devices as a natural part of their lives. Despite this, few of them understand the technical workings of laptops, tablets, smartphones, interactive whiteboards etc. Most of them merely apply their basic functions and use them to interact on social networks.

One institution that has had difficulties keeping pace with these new developments is the education system – and schools are undoubtedly still struggling, at least from what can be observed in Germany. German as well as international studies such as the International Computer and Information Literacy Study in 2013 have attested only average digital literacy among German pupils.[16] Some older teachers learned their profession without using a computer and even the younger ones are not necessarily being prepared properly for the digital classroom though their training, even though the technical equipment is available in most schools. A fact that makes it even more difficult to address the challenge of digitalisation in schools in Germany is that education is managed at each state rather than at the federal level. For example, in the federal state of Lower Saxony, many schools did not even offer ICT as a school subject until recently and in most states, the subject remains optional.

With this paradox in mind, the German non-profit organisation Wissenschaft im Dialog and the Klaus Tschira Foundation came together to discuss what could be done to support teachers and school children to teach and develop digital literacy, and particularly to prepare students for the new developments and modus operandi of today's workplace.

The idea of bringing hackdays (or hackathons) – an event format that is used in many branches to generate innovative ideas – into schools was soon born. Wissenschaft im Dialog had experience organising hackathons for adults including programmers, city planners and designers who knew what to expect when attending such an event. The aims of setting up this new project for schools were:

- To motivate students to become more digitally competent.

- To develop students' problem-solving skills and the ability to apply them.

- To provide students and teachers with an insight into current research through lightning talks.

- To establish hackdays as a working and learning method in schools.

- To encourage students to identify themselves more strongly with their school.

The conditions for *Make your school* – A creative tech workshop were created. The main question in the project design was: What is required to successfully run hackdays within the structural and local confines of German schools with participants who yet do not have professional knowledge to contribute?

Make it start: how we began

With the financial support of the Klaus Tschira Foundation, we started with a pilot phase in the 2016/2017 school year during which five schools tested the two or three-day event format and ran the events independently with support from the Make Your School team. The overall task for the students was to generate ideas that could provide tangible improvements or assets to school life. Ahead of the first hackdays we assumed that:

- The traditional time allocation for a hackathon does not fit into a school day, so we chose the term hackday.

- Since school students have less prior knowledge than adults do, they need more support. To provide this we sought mentors, mainly university students studying ICT or engineering, to provide assistance.

- To build a prototype based on the students' ideas, the schools needed a budget to purchase materials.

After the first five hackdays the project team and advisory board concluded that:

- Teachers require accurate and extensive guidance to organise hackdays as this is not part of their everyday school routine.

- School students need guidance through the process of developing their ideas.

- They need to be given examples of what can be developed.

- Simply purchasing materials ahead of an event is a waste of resources, as many of them remain unused because of the event's spontaneous nature (see 'Make it happen'). Our solution was to develop a toolkit of standard materials to be sent to each school event and returned to us afterwards for restocking.

- The school students need to be given basic management tools when entering the hacking phase to organise themselves and to assign tasks within their teams.

- Most hackathons have a competitive nature and end with an award ceremony for the best hack. In all pilot schools, this had an opposite effect to what we had expected: most pupils were disappointed.

Make it happen: the hackdays

Roughly speaking, our three-day hackdays are divided into three different phases: The opening and brainstorming, the hacking and the presentation of prototypes. *Make Your School* hackdays require the collaborative efforts of two to three teachers to make sure a supervisor is present at all times. Parts of the event format incorporate aspects of the design thinking method. However, the focus of *Make Your School* hackdays lies on the hacking process using digital devices and electronics.

1. Opening and brainstorming

The principal or a teacher who explains to the students why they are taking part in the project holds the opening. A member of our team also briefly explains the project. In the next step, the mentors explain the idea of the hackdays more deeply and display students' prototypes from previous hackdays. They explain the programme, the roles of the students, mentors and teachers, and the event rules. Subsequently, each mentor introduces her- or himself, including his or her academic background and working experience.

The most structured part of the event is the brainstorming, moderated by a mentor. They start by explaining the challenge: how can the students develop something new, meaningful and exciting for their school? The students split up into groups of their own choice. They reflect on their habits in daily school life using a user journey poster as a tool to identify challenges. Additional questions are used to provide inspiration to think outside the box. The mentors continue by presenting a key component of Make Your School hackdays: the contents of the material box, which contains sensors, actuators and many other electronic components. Specially designed material cards display each component and show how they can be combined, so that the pupils can plan their hacks independently, solving their problems and challenges themselves. The printed material cards are supplemented by our online database which provides further information on each material.[17] Then it is the pupils' turn again. They use sticky notes to gather ideas on how they can address the problems and challenges they have identified. In the next step they cluster and prioritise in the teams by marking them with sticky dots. They document the ideas with the best ratings using the idea template provided and present them to the whole group. Again, the mentors cluster the ideas to identify whether similar ideas can be combined. At the end of this session the students can decide which hack they would like to work on – the mentors ensure that the teams are not too large.

2. The hacking

The hacking is the most flexible part of the hackdays. At this point, the students start to work independently in teams, identify features of their hack and their own abilities, develop a project plan with milestones, structure their teamwork, assign tasks, hold brief interim presentations and build their prototype. The different teams may have different work stages in the hacking phase, depending on what they have agreed on. The mentors visit every team regularly to make sure they are not stuck with any of their tasks. They support them with conceptual hints, links to online tutorials, and assist them when they have technical problems. The mentors do not tell the students what to do; instead, they help them to find solutions themselves.

Once each team has defined what they need to do for their prototype, they set up their workspace with e.g. soldering stations or saws depending on which equipment and processes they plan to use. At this point, the pupils get to know the material boxes. Their main tasks during the hacking phase is to experiment, analyse, discard failed attempts and continue with successful ones: a typical trial and error process that the students document for themselves and for their presentation. If any of the material they need is not available in the material box, the teams add it to a shopping list so that one of the teachers can purchase additional material on the same day.

An optional part of the programme is a lightning talk given by an external expert. This interruption can be a good opportunity to bring the whole group back together and provide information about how the experts started their career, e.g. explaining how they built a prototype once and how they continued their work.

3. The presentation

The final phase is the presentation of the prototypes from each team, which can either be presented in a series of lecture-style demonstrations or a fair. The students explain their prototypes to other teams, teachers and visitors either via a presentation with a document camera, pictures or videos; or by presenting it at their fair stand. Regardless of the presentation format, students prepare for the presentation at the end of the hacking phase. The actual presentation starts with a short welcome of all guests by either a teacher, the school principal or a mentor. A slide show of the hackdays helps the guests understand the process the students have used to design their hacks and gives them a sense of the working atmosphere. When the students explain their hack, they outline the challenge they have identified, their motivation to work on this hack and the aims they had. In addition, the pupils share their experiences.

Make Your School is subject to scientific monitoring to ensure quality and that it meets current standards. The Technische Universität Braunschweig began monitoring *Make Your School* in February 2018. Francine Meyer is investigating the effectiveness of the hackdays at schools as part of her doctoral work, under the supervision of Professor Dr Monika Taddicken in the Department of Communication and Media Science.

Make it work: teacher and mentor trainings

To ensure the hackdays run smoothly, both teachers and mentors are essential. For this reason, we offer trainings for both players. In fact, attending a training session is compulsory for participating in the project.

The teachers gain insight into what needs to be organised and into the hackdays as the core element. They experiment with hacking themselves on a small scale and are given examples and ideas of how they can make the impact of the hackdays last. *Make Your School* also provides a handbook, which guides the teachers through their preparations and gives advice on the hackdays.

During their training, we introduce the mentors to the project, its stakeholders, its participants and the working method used during hackdays. They also learn more on their role as a mentor, which include guiding and moderating the pupils through the hackday process. To understand the process, the mentors participate in a structured brainstorming process so that they can experience the activity from the pupils' perspective. They also practise guiding others through such a process. The mentors are also trained on how to effectively interact with students and teachers while considering the unique dynamics of the schools.

Material box and cards

The material box is the heart of the project. It includes the following components:

Physical computing	Controllers	Arduinos, Raspberry Pis
	Sensors	Temperature, humidity, light
	Actuators	Multiphase motors, pumps, fans
	Communication	GPS, RFID
	User interface	Number pads, switches, LEDs
	Shields, drivers	Amplifiers, potential dividers
	Electricity	Batteries, power adapters
	Connections	Battery holders, cables, lustre terminals, HDMI
	Memory	SD cards
Building material	Construction	Screws, squares, nails
	Electrical engineering	Resistors, capacitors

Tools	Construction	Soldering irons, electrical engineering & fine mechanics-set
	Electrical engineering	Scissors, hammer, saw
	Working safety	safety glasses and gloves
Infrastructure	Autarky	WLAN-LTE router, extension cables
	Software tools	MIT app inventor 2, arduino DIE, python
Workshop materials		Post its, pens, sticky dots, USB sticks, User Journey Poster, idea templates

We send material boxes to each school that runs hackdays. The school returns it afterwards. The pupils take out and keep what they need for their hacking projects. We restock the boxes for the next school.

The material cards help the pupils to identify the elements in the box and find out which components can be combined in certain ways. On the front of each card there is a picture of the component, its name and assigned number. On the back is a brief description of the unit and a link to our website for a more detailed description plus further links to tutorials and information about the components' functions.

The colours and symbols on the front of the card indicate how the cards and thus the components can be connected like dominoes. If two cards can be connected, so can the two components. The symbols display how the components can communicate. The material cards come with a key card that explains how to use them. The cards not only help the pupils to understand what the material box contains; they also help them to plan their hack and check which components are compatible. This way they can explore what they need to implement in their hack independently at the beginning of the hacking phase.

Make it last: maker festivals and local networks

A key focus for the future of the *Make Your School* project is making the impact of the hackdays last. One aspect of this is encouraging students to continue working on their hacks and apply to participate in our annual maker festival. Our second strategy will be to support schools by building up local networks of companies, professional associations, maker spaces and other relevant stakeholders to lay the foundations for:

- Receiving material support to set up a makerspace in the school.

- Helping the students to continue their work on the hacks by providing professional knowledge and materials.

- Involving the stakeholders in the hackdays e.g. engineers as lecturers for lightning talks or for providing support when the students continue to work on their hacks.

- Finding companies and professional associations to support school hackdays financially in the future.

Make it spread: hints for running school hackdays

We are aware that the way we run *Make Your School* hackdays is very cost and time intensive. We could not realise the project without the dedicated and generous support of the Klaus Tschira Foundation. Resources – both costs and time – are very limited in schools and we rely on teachers who are committed to the project and are passionate about providing their students with new insights from outside school life. We highly appreciate their dedicated work and time!

Our goal in the next two to three years is to enable the schools to work more independently once they have set up their local networks. That will make it possible for us to involve more schools throughout Germany and to spread the knowledge that teachers need to run hackdays.

Although our project has required considerable resources to reach its goals, we do think it is possible to run hackdays on a lower budget. If you are interested in running your own hackdays, here are our tips:

- Organisation: We are happy to provide suggestions (including for international colleagues) about how to run local hackdays including advice on the programme, roles, and resources such as materials and locations.

- Programme: We have a set programme for our hackdays, loosely based on hackathons. It can easily be adapted to your local needs. Do not hesitate to contact us.

- Materials: In Germany, several organisations and companies provide free components such as micro controllers, shields, actuators or sensors and even courses for teachers. Find out if there are similar opportunities in your local area and set up your own material box.

- Professional knowledge: Paid mentors are the most expensive part of our hackdays. You could try to replace them with volunteers such as professional engineers, apprentices from local companies, or members of local makerspaces. Companies and professional associations might also sponsor parts of your material box. Get in touch with them. We believe that with a local network you could move mountains for your students.

Brainstorming on how to overcome the challenges[18]

The hacking[19]

Group presentations[20]

Chapter 12

Establishing a Fablab: Fostering Local Creativity

Martin Oloo

In 2008, I moved to the capital city of Nairobi to undertake my social work studies full-time. There, I was later invited by Arc Kenya to join the board of directors (BoD). I was later elected as the Chairman of the BoD. At Arc Kenya, I was part of establishing the first fablab in Kenya named ARO fablab. It was located in a remote area of Western Kenya. Arc Kenya, had been working with the community by encouraging community-based interventions. The initiator and chief fundraiser for Arc Kenya – Kjellan Spinnangr, had a vision of fablabs being able to support people from disadvantaged backgrounds in creating things by themselves and thus participate in improving the local economy. The idea was initially very advanced for a remote village with underdeveloped basic infrastructure. ARO fablab received funding for five years and was set up in July 2007, but it closed once funding ceased. As a board member, I saw the fablab struggling to survive due to acute staffing shortages. I decided to take a risk and asked the BoD if they could allow me to take charge of the fablab to revive it. Various challenges loomed, including:

1. My educational and professional background focused on social work;

2. My financial situation, lack of networks, and support;

3. My initial belief that developing a fablab would be a difficult venture;

4. The Arc Kenya partners did not support the fablab idea.

I established a small committee of friends who helped me to analyse the situation and write an evaluation report. Among other things, some of the major challenges and corresponding recommendations included:

Challenge	Recommendation
Location – in a remote place	The fablab should be easily accessible, more so by the students. It should be situated in a town with good infrastructure, including electricity and internet.
Fundraising	A need for new registration to allow new partners for resource mobilisation.
Management and productivity	Getting more machines and delivering the right training; Aro fablab had only a Modela milling machine, vinyl cutter, and a laser cutter. All were faulty. For a completely functional fablab, there was a need for additional machines like a 3D printer, Computer Numeric Control (CNC) router, hand tools, and other equipment. The right skills were needed for the operators of the fablab, such as having a background in engineering, design, or computer science.

I then contacted Kjellan who supported our findings and managed to raise 4,000 USD for us to start. On 1 September 2015, we reopened with one employee with a background in electronic engineering. I was still working full-time at my other job but one month later, I decided to resign and accepted a full-time job in the fablab. During this period, I also contacted the Fab foundation to enquire how they could support me to revive this fablab. Among my requests were skills training, additional equipment, and hand tools plus a cash grant. Fablab President Sherry Lassiter was very supportive throughout the whole process.

I was given a scholarship to join the Fab Academy and in January 2016, I had to move to Nairobi at Gearbox. Surprisingly, I became the first Kenyan to graduate from this 20-week digital fabrication course. In early August, I joined the Fablabbers at an annual global conference in Shenzhen China. Here, I was able to meet different makers, innovators, entrepreneurs, and potential partners. I had an intensive meeting with the Fab Foundation president, accompanied by a trainer who had become a very close friend after meeting at this conference for the first time. At our meeting, we agreed that the Fab Foundation would send us a few machines. But things did not work as planned. My Organisation disagreed with my proposal of relocation and re-registration of the fablab and I was left with no option but to start a new fablab.

The birth of fablab Winam

I started discussing fablabs with youths in small meetings and any forum I could attend. I also informed the Fab Foundation and they agreed to support the new initiative with machines, however, I was told that I would be responsible for any costs after shipping. It took me a long time to get funds for the clearance at the customs. I eventually formed a community-based organisation called Winam Innovators Community Based Organisation (CBO) with some youths. Keeping them was never easy since they needed quick results but that was not forthcoming. Through a friend I met on a bus, I was introduced to Africa's Talking. Africa's Talking is an organisation that ensures that the developer community in Africa is successful at creating, growing, and sustaining great businesses, using our solutions. They aim to support a viable, entrepreneurial ecosystem for Africa. It currently works in over ten African countries with its headquarters based in Nairobi Kenya. They believe that with this mission, they will be able to support a viable, entrepreneurial ecosystem for Africa. Later, Africa's Talking created AT-Labs - a subsidiary company tasked with supporting developers and entrepreneurs with the hope of creating several African made companies. Currently, there are about ten such companies incubated under AT-Labs - fablab Winam is one.

I used to talk to everyone I met about the fablab idea and explained the challenges we faced. I was in the town service bus in Nairobi heading to the Ideation workshop at the Dalberg offices and I was not sure of my bus stop so I started a conversation with the lady sitting next to me, asking her to notify me when we reached the stop. She asked where I was going to. Coincidentally, her office was in the same building as the office I was heading to. I explained to her what I worked on and the challenges we have. She said, "I wish our CEO was around so that you can tell him about your dream". She then took me to her office (Africa's Talking) to show me around and we agreed that she would inform me when the CEO was around. At last, I was invited to meet him. I contacted my team in Nairobi about this and we went for our first meeting - by coincidence an individual from my team worked there too and became very instrumental in handling our communications. The meeting went well and they looked impressed but weren't sure how to help us. We had three such meetings and finally I could hear the CFO asking us for the details of the customs and the clearance and forwarding agent, which I did very fast! At first, I thought that they were just helping us to pay for the customs duty but then they said that they would like to take us in as one of their incubatee companies.

Why I tried this approach and what I considered as I designed it

In establishing fablab Winam, I insisted that I wanted it in Kisumu even though many people had tried to give me offers of support if I would take it to their places of choice like Nairobi, Mombasa, and Eldoret among other offers. I was born and raised in the Western Kenya region and I have seen many young people struggling with their ideas but not reaching anywhere. This region is known to produce the best Fundi's (artisans) - carpenters, mechanics, tailors etc. These talents are now dying because many young people go to school to earn a degree then desperately look for jobs which are never there and finally accept 'just any job', which limits their potential. After graduation, many end up riding motorbikes for transportation but a good number find themselves in gang robberies and drug abuse. Several are also migrating to Nairobi city believing they will get opportunities since all companies and tech services are based there. The universities and other colleges are too exam-oriented and many graduates (even those with technical courses) do not acquire the desired hands-on skills. I believed that a fablab would provide the space for these young people to get hands-on experience while building purposeful things. I believed that in fablabs they would be challenged to think critically and be active in solving challenges. Africa has several problems, and all these are opportunities if solutions are built around them.

Kisumu city is one of three Kenyan cities located in the Western Kenya region. It sits at the border of Tanzania and Uganda the city also acts as a port to Lake Victoria. It has been independent and left behind in development due to political reasons. It has always been perceived to be a zone of opposition and so no opportunities are available. It has no major industries. Investors often shun it and it has been dominated by NGOs which lately have reduced their services. It has the highest rates of HIV/AIDS in Kenya and poverty is very high. Some of the best brains and leaders have links to this region, such as the late Tom Mboya, the late Oginga Odinga, the father of former President of the United States of America Barack Obama, Kenya's Former Prime Minister Raila Odinga, Lupita Nyongo a Hollywood actress, among others.

Nairobi is overcrowded and I believe that if the people from Kisumu make good use of our fablab, we shall see several cottage manufacturing industries being established and youths will be able to take responsibility for creating their own future.

We use a learning approach focused on making a link with the craft industry (and not only about digital making). The approach we took was not an easy one since it needed many resources, including appropriately skilled people and funds for both machines and operations. As stated earlier, people consider Nairobi as a hub of opportunities and any young educated individual will move to Nairobi, leaving the old and less educated behind in villages to work on farms as well as other less prestigious odd-jobs. We want to give opportunities to less privileged individuals.

The fablab has been instrumental for the local community in the areas of innovation, entrepreneurship, and youth empowerment. This was achieved by creating a maker's hub where different individuals in the local community can access digital fabrication machines.

Fablab Winam has also created a knowledge sharing hub where different professionals in different fields have brainstorming sessions to identify solutions to locally existing problems. Currently, projects achieved through brainstorming emphasise the need for a platform where different workers showcase their skills and abilities, while individuals looking for such services can utilise the platform.

Fablab Winam has also been a source of livelihood for individuals within the locality. The lab has five employees, namely a manager, an accountant, a workshop technician, and an electrical technician. It also offers internship opportunities which improves the employability chances of graduates. A few institutions have also identified it as a resource centre for tech challenges. They see it as a place where answers can be given by users and professionals available outside the scope of those who are employed within the organisation. The lab has created a source of income for interior designers and Jua Kali artisans; these artisans have improved their skills in fabrication and are now able to achieve a greater finish on their designs. Therefore, they sell their products at increased prices leading to increased income.

Fablab Winam has also improved the proficiency of local trainers in local polytechnics in the region, through providing training for the instructors on different digital fabrication techniques. The students get a glimpse of modern fabrication techniques which are not included in their curriculum.

The fablab also facilitates monthly bootcamps that are aimed at educating young people on entrepreneurship and innovation. This event provides a networking opportunity for different innovators in the local region; some events also involve top government officials who aid in providing information on viable opportunities for innovators as well as providing crucial input for different innovations that are showcased.

The younger generation within the region is also not left out. Fablab Winam organises the Fab Children programme that is aimed at introducing and strengthening STEAM subjects to children. The programme provides them with a glimpse of practical hands-on skills as well as giving them a peek into the world of innovation and the fablab environment at the earliest age. Currently, plans are underway to introduce the programmes in local schools to widen our outreach.

What we do

We are a hub for knowledge-share, skills and digital fabrication, empowering the community through local manufacturing and human-centred design. Fablab Winam's vision is community empowerment through innovation and local manufacturing. Our mission is to provide a prototyping space for nurturing innovation and entrepreneurship. Our values are collaboration, innovation, accountability, professionalism, and integrity.

Our current programmes and activities include:

1. Innopreneur bootcamp;

2. Fab Kids;

3. Fab Academy;

4. Trainings;

5. Fabrications (prototyping);

6. Mentorship (incubation/ start-up support);

7. Contracting.

Innopreneur Bootcamp

This is a monthly gathering of makers, innovators, entrepreneurs and all other players in the ecosystem going through a learning session of idea to market with a theme for each month. The main purpose of these meetings is to sensitise makers to the opportunities available at the fablab, creating a networking platform for them, marking different players in the ecosystem, and lastly to help build momentum towards the planned Western Kenya region innovation week. To date, we have held four successful bootcamps, and we use them to raise awareness about our activities to various leaders.

To assess the success of the Innopreneur bootcamp, we use the following criteria: attendance against invitation; delivery of the day's topic, and the level of involvement of the audience, either in practicals or their contributions etc. To attain this success, one must adequately prepare, ranging from assessing the learning needs of participants, preparation of the lesson practicals, event funding, chief guest identification, to invitation and confirmation acquisition. We have been privileged to host the National Chairman of the Youth Enterprise Development Fund as the chief guest and the Deputy British High Commissioner. As a result, the usage of the fablab has increased since more people call or visit, make inquiries, or seek services. The fablab's network with the ecosystem has increased together with conversation on making.

FabKids

This is a collaborative activity where children are introduced to science, technology, engineering, arts, and mathematics (STEAM) at an early age. They learn and build things together locally but in collaboration with children in another fablab in another country. For example, fablab Winam and fablab Argentina might collaborate in an activity where the children will be allowed to see each other and wave to each other via video conferencing before starting. They are given the same instructions then start the activity at the same time. This is viewed to bridge the global difference brought about by location. We conduct this programme with a Latin American network called FabLat Children (I first saw a Facebook post of FabKids when I was still completing the Fab Academy course early 2016, I then started the conversation by inboxing them. Alejandra Diaz De Leon, who is the co-founder of the organisation, and I kept the conversation going until we met physically in Shenzhen China during the Global Fab Conference in August. In 2017, during another conference in Santiago Chile, I participated in the first FabKids activity. We discussed the collaboration in-depth awaiting the establishment of my fablab. FabLat Children comprises of people with varied professional backgrounds. We share documents using google drive, discuss successes, challenges, good practices and recommendations for new trials. Among the children's programmes delivered include Emosilla (for making chairs which are cut by CNC router), Fab Lamps, Drawbots (introducing electronics), and Fab Toys (using 3D printers to print customised toys). We are incorporating African arts in the syllabus so we can use this platform to teach and preserve the rich African cultural arts and practices. We piloted the first session in December which lasted two days and the results were impressive.

The two activities were creating hanging gardens for day one and Emosilla for the last day. For the hanging gardens activity, the children were able to recycle water bottles, cut them, prepare soil for planting, plant, water and hang them along the walls. This was meant to help them appreciate agriculture which can be done in different ways, while creating awareness of waste recycling and maintaining the environment. For the Emosilla (emotional chair), the children were provided with cut parts which they then assembled. They also explored emotions and drew a facial expression which conveyed their emotions. These were transferred digitally, then engraved on a piece of plywood which then was pasted on the back of the seat. They then proceeded to colour them to their taste. This was the most creative day and they liked it. It tested their skills on team-work, connection of patterns, and painting. They were supposed to carry them home, but this did not happen. We believe that this process took the children through a process of thinking and creating things with fun. It made them own both the process and the product. They demanded more time and activities but due to the plan and resources, we could not provide that.

Fab Academy

This is a 20-week global massive open online course (MOOC) delivered by the Fab Academy[21] teaching the principles and practices of digital fabrication. The students must be in a given fablab (node) which is equipped with relevant equipment and hand tools and has a local instructor. fablab Winam is hosting this training for the first time. Two other fablabs in Africa host it in Rwanda and Egypt. We have five students, one of whom came from the Democratic Republic of the Congo. The course normally costs 5,000 USD but fablab Winam chose to reduce the fee to 4,000 USD but still no student could afford it. We managed to get a scholarship offer from the Fab Foundation[22] for the five students. Upon completion, students will be equipped with all round hands-on skills together with project management and documentation experience.

Training

We also run training for individuals and institutions on various areas including 3D printing, laser cutting, CNC routing, printed circuit board (PCB), production, electronics, vinyl cutting, coding, Computer Aided Designing (CAD), Computer Aided Manufacturing (CAM) and arts among others. These help empower users on the right skills they need to execute their work. We work closely with some technical institutions to support them in trying local productions and even using some of the machines they have but have never used. Here we target high school leavers, tech enthusiasts, college students, artisans, and entrepreneurs. We have trained several people in this. We are also currently working with two technical institutions on organising training for them.

Fabrications (prototyping)

Here we help people to produce parts of the projects they are working on during prototyping. We work with them in project designing, raising bills of materials (BOM) and using the available tools, we produce parts. We do this to both of our regular users and one-time clients who might be working on their projects elsewhere. We currently work with some interior designers under this. We are also keen on involving local artisans (*jua kali*) since they have always fabricated things to ensure products are ready for the general market.

Mentorship (incubation / start-up support)

This is our core business, however, it has not been exploited as much as we hoped to since we have not found 'ideal' start-ups, nor the resources to do so. We will be able to take the start-ups and incubatees through a design thinking process, other necessary areas including monetisation, talent recruitment, and intellectual property protection.

Contracting

We hope to be contracted by other companies, organisations, and individuals to conduct work for them depending on their needs. We recently worked with one new beach restaurant to support them in setting up and branding.

Lessons learned

Establishing a fablab (especially if you want it to be independent) is an uphill task and it comes with several lessons:

- Vision bearing is a big task and needs a lot of perseverance, resilience, determination and unmeasured passion.

- Organising people and rallying them to support your vision is difficult but it is much harder keeping them focused and motivated. I was able to keep constant and open communication with stakeholders, know when to hold on, and when to move on. Failing to get help from anyone does not destroy your relationship with them.

- Starting/founding a company involves many sacrifices but it provides many positive experiences such as improved communication, management skills, and resilience.

- Networking and collaboration are key to any success.

- Acquiring the right skills, experiences, and resources are vital in achieving success. Nevertheless, being passionate, and determined to achieve your vision is vital.

Chapter 13

Designing Open Learning Challenges

Jenny Kostka

When I decided to become a teacher, it was not because I love working with children, or the idea of inspiring future generations. It was because I love physics. I wanted to introduce students to physics and get them to love it too, which was daunting; as a school subject, physics does not have a great reputation. On the first day, I would always ask my students what their expectations for the class were, and I would get replies containing phrases like "lots of maths", "difficult", or "scary".

But physics, and science in general, has another side. It is not all about – not even mostly about – solving word problems with pages and pages of calculations. It is a way of understanding the world, and of expressing creativity. This is the piece that gets left out the most: that being scientific is not the opposite of being creative, science *is* a creative pursuit. Over the years, I have pushed my curriculum away from the scripted lab exercises that I had been taught and toward more opportunities for students to design their own experiments and to make things like bumper cars when studying momentum or Rube Goldberg devices to learn about energy.

My own learning about constructionism and the work of Seymour Papert made me want to push this idea even further – in addition to incorporating these more targeted design experiences into my class, I wanted to complete a full-on, open-ended constructionist project. I wanted to allow students to follow their own interests and give them time and space to learn by making something of their own choosing.

My AP Physics class was the perfect setting for these constructionist projects. This may seem counterintuitive; the stereotype of AP classes is that they have a rigid, standardised curriculum. This is not completely true – yes, the standards that need to be taught (and the exam) are well-defined, and the syllabus needs to be submitted and approved, but there is room for teachers to create their own structure and materials. Crucially for me, there is usually a big gap between the date of the exam (early May) and the end of the school year (in my case, late June). This gap was the ideal place for me and my students to do an open-ended, interest-based maker project.

I was especially fortunate in the structure and culture of the school in which I was teaching. South Shore Charter Public School was founded in 1995, one of the first charter schools in Massachusetts, with a philosophy based around project-based learning. Student-led projects (in grades K-

8) and workshops (in grades 9-12) have been a big part of the school from the beginning. The students with whom I did these projects were 11th-graders, and several of them had been at the school since the elementary grades. We had also been learning through smaller projects throughout the year, so these longer and more open-ended projects were a natural extension of what we had already been doing, and for some of them, what they had been doing throughout their entire school career.

Project design and project focus

I did this project with a class of eight students (the number was so small because AP physics was a mixed 11th/12th grade class, and the 12th-graders spent the last six weeks of the school year at off-campus internships.) The project was deliberately open-ended, with me in a facilitator role. We were not exploring a single topic together – instead, students were free to follow their own interests, and my only requirements were that they had to make something and connect what they made to a physics topic we had learned during the year. Instead of adding a new topic to the course (which I had done in previous years of teaching AP physics), I allowed them to go back to something we had done before. The pace of an AP course does not allow for spending more than a few weeks on any particular topic, so my hope was that they would identify something that had sparked their interest over the course of the year and dive more deeply into it. To that end, I gave them this prompt:

Make something that interests you, that you will enjoy making, and that challenges you. Your project must include a connection to a physics topic, about which you will include some research.

Once the big decision of the overall focus of the project was made, there were several other decisions to consider in the project design.

Assessment

I started by thinking about what I wanted them to produce, and how I wanted to assess it. I knew I wanted them to make something, but did I want to assess the actual thing they made? How would that even work, if all the projects were different? I had used standards-based grading all year, with standards that were divided into categories by topic, plus a category that encompassed lab and scientific thinking skills. None of these, however, would really work for this project – the topics would presumably all be different, and while collecting lab-style data might be part of the process for some students, it was not really what the project was about. I knew I had to come up with a new category of standards. In writing these new standards, I thought: *What would be common to all the projects? What did I want to see students doing, no matter what their topic was?* The answers to those questions did not have much to do with physics content, although I did want to see them connecting to it. Rather, they were things like troubleshooting effectively, documenting their process, presenting their work, and reflecting on what they were learning. I put these standards into the rubric format we had been using all year and gave them that rubric at the outset of the project.

Product

Since all the projects would be different, I focused on the documentation and presentation as the vehicle for this assessment. From my own experience in making things and documenting progress through photos, design journals, and blogs, I know that how you show what you are working on can be wildly varied and extremely personal, and if a method is not working for you, you will not keep up with it. I tried to make the requirements for documentation as open-ended as the project. I did not develop a form or checklist, nor choose a format for them. I did require that it had to be digital for ease of sharing (although I told them they could do everything on paper and photograph/scan it if they preferred paper), and I had a list of things I wanted included in the documentation, like a description of their original intent and a summary of their physics research. In the end, all three of the groups – again, a small sample size – chose to use a combination of Google slides and docs (a pdf of all the instructions (prompt, requirements, and rubric) is available).[23]

Resources

The last thing to consider before starting the project was the resources I had at my disposal. As a science/engineering teacher, my room is always full of stuff. At the beginning and end of the year, when setting or packing up, I am often jealous of the teachers who can fit all their things into just a few boxes, but during the year I love my overflowing shelves and storage units. I had lab equipment, electronics equipment, hardware, and hand tools, plus plenty of cardboard, Styrofoam, scraps of wood, and other miscellaneous stuff I have collected over the years. I put all of that at my students' disposal. I was also lucky enough to have a budget structure where teachers could request funds for things throughout the year as needed, instead of only once a year. If my students needed something I did not already have, which was the case for some of them, they were able to request it. This was a bit of a mixed blessing, though, because requesting something through the school meant ordering it through the school, with all the attendant paperwork, and some groups spent a lot of time waiting for materials to arrive.

I also had to consider what we could realistically and safely do in the classroom. My students were all 16-17 years old, and I had plenty of goggles, safety gloves, and understanding colleagues, but some things had to be off-limits. I said no to spray painting, testing an air cannon, and bringing in a table saw. I said yes to testing a catapult (in an open space) and bringing in a router. I rolled my eyes at the repeated requests for explosions. I made many small judgment calls, every day, and thankfully no one was injured.

Class structure

A constructionist project is going to be somewhat chaotic. I have never had the kind of classroom where students sit in quiet rows, taking notes on everything I said at the front of the room, but I knew these projects would still be a step beyond our usual level of chaos. This meant that I had to add some structures to the project, both at the beginning and throughout the work, to keep things productive and moving forward.

Idea generation and research

My biggest worry, from experience with projects, was that students would decide on what they were going to make – often something they had seen someone else make – in the first five minutes and remain focused on that the entire time. While decision-making and focus did not sound like negative things, the pitfall I had seen students fall into was trying to reproduce a cool project they had seen online rather than starting with a more general idea for what they wanted to make or a topic they wanted to explore. I hoped the requirement for connection to a physics topic would help to prevent this, but I also emphasised exploration at the beginning. The first few days of the project were designated for looking at many different sources, from their physics notes and our Google Classroom page to sites like Instructables,[24] Make,[25] and Thingiverse.[26] I did not let them tell me what their project was going to be until they had spent some time poking around, and I repeated *ad nauseam* that their starting point should be their interests and they should be looking for inspiration, not instructions. Did some of them still choose a project right away? Yes, they did. But at least they had some sense of what is out there and where to look for ideas.

I also knew it would be important to provide resources throughout the project and to nudge them toward productive ways of using them. The school is not one-on-one with technology, but I made sure a few laptops were always available. I reminded them of the "ask three before me" guideline – the three in this case being Google, YouTube, and their classmates. When students did inevitably come to me with questions, I asked them some of my own, like *What solutions for this problem have you already tried? What do you think you could search for to find out more about this?* or *What is your project doing, and what do you want it to be doing?* I tried very hard not to give them too much help or simple answers to things, but to push them toward thinking through problems, searching for help, and debugging their projects. This is always the hardest part, because if I can see what is going wrong and how to fix it, I want to jump in. However, I know they will learn so much more by researching and getting themselves unstuck, so I made a very conscious effort to let that productive struggle happen.

Timeline and check-ins

There is a difference, though, between struggling and floundering. Another part of my role as facilitator was to give them some checkpoints and monitor their progress. The checkpoints I established were very general: the project was about six weeks long, so I told them that the first week should be about exploration, the last week should be about putting together the presentation of their project, and the time in between was theirs to focus on the making itself. These were not, of course, hard-and-fast rules – exploring other ideas and organising things for the presentation happened throughout the project, but it was helpful to have some rough structure.

The monitoring piece was more crucial. This happened both informally through observation and daily conversations, and with pre-planned weekly check-ins. Each week, I sat down with each group and asked them to tell me about their progress, then took notes on what they said. Even though I was in the room with them the whole time and had seen their progress, I think it was helpful for both me and the students to have them articulate it. During these check-ins, I asked two main questions: *What did you do this week?* and *What do you need to do next?* The conversation and any further questions followed from the responses to those two, and the notes all went into one big spreadsheet that was shared with the whole class. With my small, relatively mature group, this was, for the most part, enough to keep things on track.

Presentation

Even though it was such a small group, I wanted to have them present their work at the end in a somewhat formal manner. What I really wanted was to have them present to members of the school community outside of our class, and I did invite others in, but the presentations ended up happening during final exams, so that did not work out. Still, each group (or individual) stood up in front of the class with their project and their documentation, and talked through what they had planned, how they had made their project, how it connected to a physics topic, and what they had learned from the process. They asked and answered questions about their work, demonstrated or showed videos of their projects in action, and talked about how they could take what they learned into other, future projects.

Results

So ... how did it all turn out? Well, the good news was that they made three ambitious projects, and they learned a great deal about troubleshooting and managing time, as well as skills like woodworking, wiring, and of course, the application of physics concepts. The (sort of) bad news was that only one of the three projects was fully completed, while the other two were more like prototypes. From my point of view, this was bad news mainly because the students found it discouraging, not because I really cared about having perfect, finished pieces.

Here's what they made:

The Galaxy Guitar

This project was made by a group of five students, spearheaded by several students who had a deep interest in music. The plan was to create an electric guitar from scratch, which would be painted with a galaxy and played by a student in his band. The only pieces they bought that were pre-made were the neck and pick-ups; they planned to carve the body from a block of ash, wire and solder everything together (maybe adding some LEDs for extra coolness) and use knobs and switches from a donor guitar. The connections to physics were partly in the circuitry, but mostly in their research about waves, resonance, harmonics, and how that connects to music.

This was the group that needed the most specialised parts, things that I did not already have, and so their progress was the most restricted by waiting for things to arrive at the school – for example, the neck did not come in until the day they presented. Because of this, they ended up with a prototype guitar with all the wiring done on a breadboard that was attached – yes, with duct tape – to the body of the donor guitar, plus a roughly carved ash body. Their

Frankenguitar was not pretty, but it was playable, and the day they got it to work was a lot of fun, with other teachers stopping by to see what the music was and (those that could play) trying it out themselves.

This group got stuck in some interesting ways, on things that were not expected to be problematic. For example, they found a pattern of the guitar body to trace, but it was too big to print on a single sheet of paper, so they ended up using a site called BlockPosters[27] to print it in sections and assemble it. The process of figuring out how to get it to the size they wanted turned out to be a good review of calculating scale. The time they spent waiting for parts gave them more time to research and make a deeper connection to the physics of sound, as well as try out smaller projects like making a vinyl-cut sticker to put on the guitar.

While they did not end up with the finished project they envisioned, I think they still benefited greatly.

The Catapult

This group was a pair of students, and they were the only ones to complete a finished project. They built a Mangonel catapult that used the tension in a twisted rope to launch small wooden and metal balls about 30 feet across the school's great room. In typical teenage fashion, they pushed the finished catapult to its limit, bringing in the strongest friends they could find to add more twist to the rope until it finally snapped.

This was also the most systematic group: they started by researching different types of catapults, building a small popsicle-stick mock-up with a pen as the throwing arm, and using it to calculate the lengths of wood and other parts they would need for the full-scale version. In contrast to the galaxy guitar group, their process was linear and they did not often get stuck on anything. Their only hindrance was in the initial testing, when they found it counterintuitive that they both had to twist the rope in the same direction to get it to build up the tension needed to fire the projectile. Due to this smooth process, they had time to experiment with different weights of projectiles and shapes of the bowl that held the projectile to try to get the most distance, as well as use that data and projectile motion equations to calculate its initial speed when leaving the catapult.

One thing this group articulated about their learning that I did not expect was a skill that was unrelated to the building or the physics involved. They had to fill out forms and email the principal to be able to buy the lumber, which they had not done before, and dealing with those administrative tasks was a skill they cited as something they would carry forward. It sounds mundane and not nearly as much fun as launching projectiles, but they were right – navigating administrative structures is something they will have to do many times in the future, and I was both surprised and happy to see them mention it.

The Master Blaster Mk.1

The last project was done by an individual student, and his goal was to build a pneumatic cannon, or a 'custom high-powered nerf gun'. The nature of the project made it difficult to do the building and testing at school, but he had his heart set on it, so I gave him the go-ahead. He ended up doing a lot of the hands-on work at home, while researching and documenting during class time. This is a tough way to work, and a big contributor to his ending up with a partially finished prototype instead of a completed project.

After researching different designs, he came up with one that was fairly straightforward: a chamber that could be pressurised through a valve at one end, with a barrel connected to another valve at the other end of the chamber, which could be released to launch the projectile.

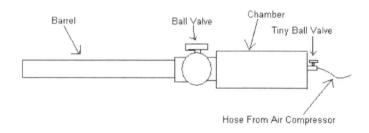

Building it and getting it to reliably become pressurised turned out to be more difficult, and most of his troubleshooting was around what parts to use and how to attach them to eliminate leaks. He ended up with a PVC chamber with the two valves and was able to stop most of the leaks, but there was some persistent leaking around the smaller valve that could not be eliminated before the deadline for the project arrived.

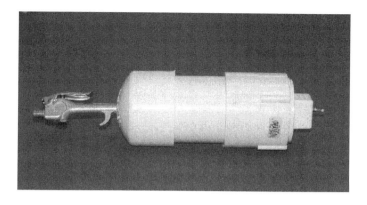

On a positive note, however, this student did more delving into new physics concepts than any other group. His plan to calculate the speed of the projectile and its acceleration in the barrel was a connection to a previous topic, but the AP Physics 1 curriculum does not include anything about fluid dynamics. His research into concepts like Pascal's Law and the relationship between the area of the air flow and its velocity were completely new to him. He concluded his presentation with plans for the Master Blaster Mk.2, so I think it is safe to say he discovered a new area of interest.

Reflection

One thing I love about teaching is how I learn new things myself. In implementing a project that was so open-ended, I learned a great deal about ambition vs practicality, managing a chaotic process, and what students can do given space and time.

The biggest takeaway for me was that I need to help students balance the desire to go big against the need to have a feasible project. I still do not think the project needs to be finished and perfect to be a success, but it is frustrating to have a big gap between what you envision and what you accomplish. If I could go back, I think I would still let the Galaxy Guitar group choose the ambitious project for which they had a passion, but I would encourage the Master Blaster student to choose something that he could work on in class, and perhaps to find a partner to share the work.

I would also make the monitoring part of the process a little – but not too much – more robust. Instead of simply checking in verbally and having students describe what they had done and needed to do, I would ask the groups to show me their documentation and reflect on it on an ongoing basis as well, in whatever form they were using. The groups sometimes fell into the all-too-common trap of getting so wrapped up in what they were doing that they did not stop to take notes or photos along the way. While I loved seeing that level of engagement, I want them to see the value of tracking what they are doing before they get to the point of putting together their presentation or figuring out how a mistake happened, when the missing documentation would be useful to have. Some groups learned that the hard way, and with a little more nudging, maybe they would not have had to.

All that said, I came away from this project with a greater appreciation and enthusiasm for constructionism, and I think my students did too. I did not think any of them came into my class because they were planning to have a career in physics, but they had the opportunity to take those physics concepts and explore them in a context that was relevant to them, use their hands and minds to apply them and make them concrete, and share their creativity and their interests with the rest of the group. That is what I hope they will take with them when they leave my class and South Shore Charter Public School.

Chapter 14

Developing the Research Skills of Pupils

Marina Gardash

Open-ended problems are associated with ambiguity. They invite multiple interpretations, where an individual finds their own 'correct' solution. These solutions can be based on the experiences of the individual or the experience of their friends and colleagues. This in turn allows for the creation of a basis for partnership, co-learning, and communication between pupils, as well as pupils and teachers in an educational institution. In this experience, I describe an open-ended inquiry-based biology project where the class investigated the viral disease, 'the flu'. During the project, we used a survey method as part of the task.

Young people today are surrounded by an ocean of fleeting information. They are constantly confronted with this vast information flow at home or in class. A problem arises: how can we teach to better prepare them for real life situations? I believe the main goal of a teacher is to create favourable conditions for the cognitive development of pupils.

The cognitive development of the child is influenced by the diversity of the cognitive space, that is, what we offer the pupil during the learning experience. This can be supported by using a variety of media technologies. This is interesting for Ukrainian pupils currently, however, it requires a lot of time and effort to master such technologies. The use of media technologies can be justified, as they can increase the engagement of pupils throughout the learning journey.

Media technologies allow you to present the supporting educational materials as a system of comprehensive documents in any given order. In this case, multiple channels of the pupils' perception are involved. It allows the facilitator to not only share information with pupils, but also support the associative learning of pupils. The imparting of educational content in the form of a multimedia presentation also reduces preparation time.

I find the creative component of open-ended tasks interesting. Pupils actively create their own educational content, based on their interactive method(s) of choice, which gives meaning to their learning and motivates pupils.

Creative tasks are tasks that contribute to more than the trivial memorisation and reproduction of information - new or original work is produced. They always contain a greater or lesser element of uncertainty and usually have several solutions.

In fact, any written assignment, whether it is an essay, abstract, or report, is a creative task, because we create something new, combine information differently, learn and consider new interesting facts, reason, reflect, and express our point of view. The creation of something new and unusual is creativity.

Pupils can be given a non-standard verbal or written assignment within the lesson, which requires them to think creatively and use their imagination.

The creation of such a task is a creative process for the teacher, because it must meet the following criteria:

- Not have a 'correct/right' or unambiguous solution;

- Be useful and interesting for pupils;

- Relate to real life;

- Broaden the horizons of pupils;

- Maximise the learning outcomes of students;

- Match the lesson topics.

If such tasks are too complicated for the pupils, then the first step is to introduce simple creative work, and over time, make the task more challenging.

Creative assignments create situations where pupils need to solve a problem on their own by applying their knowledge from different branches of science (and other subjects). Such tasks develop many important social skills, for example, self-expression in society, empathy, and teamwork. This creates the ideal conditions for the pupils' spiritual, moral, social, cultural, and intellectual development.

This section will now elaborate on the survey methods used by the pupils as an element of a creative assignment for pupils.

Interviewing methods can include conversations, interviews and questionnaires. Conversations can be used to obtain or clarify information during the discussion of a topic. For example, conducting a conversation with an epidemiologist about an influenza epidemic in a city or chickenpox in a nursery can serve as the basis for further report writing for a biology lesson.

The conversation can be held according to a plan where issues requiring clarification are identified. It can be conducted in free form without recording the answers of the interlocutor.

A discussion introduced into pedagogy from sociology is interviewing. During an interview, the researcher can keep to predetermined questions asked in a sequence. During the interview, responses are recorded openly.

Interviews can be divided into the following groups according to their content:

Documentary interviews

A study of events that occurred in the past, more defined facts, and interviews of opinions. The purpose of all this is to evaluate and determine views, opinions, reasoning, etc. An interview of thoughts is the most well-known form of interview. For such an interview, the goal is to evaluate and determine views, opinions, and discussions on a specific issue. For this interview, the goal is to clarify the respondent's point of view on a particular issue through listening to and processing thoughts. Conversations and interviews can be conducted face-to-face.

In the context of an interview, it is difficult to get a full interview from a 'press conference'. Usually this is a speech on a specific topic where the interviewer can get a comment on an event.

Questions for interviewing can be formulated in different ways:

- When listening to new content on the topic of the lesson; or
- for a lesson on his/her topic, when studying sources.

For example, a topic for an interview in biology might sound like this: "Vitamins are not food and not medicine, but we cannot live without them", but in chemistry "What kind of water do we drink?"

Survey

A method of mass information gathering using a questionnaire. Those to whom the questionnaires are addressed give written answers to the questions. Surveys are referred to as correspondence surveys. The questioning theme can focus on any topic such as a habit, ecological condition in the city and region, opinion on the principles of proper nutrition, etc. Having processed the answers received, pupils can process the data and present diagrams and graphs for consideration in the lesson. This allows them to analyse the main problems on this topic.

The effectiveness of the conversation, interviewing, and questioning largely depends on the content and structure of the questions asked. The conversation plan, interviews, and questionnaires involve a list of questions. The development of the questionnaire involves determining the nature of the information that needs to be obtained, carefully wording a set of questions to be asked, drawing up the first plan of the questionnaire and carrying out a trial study of it, and editing the questionnaire to its final version.

There are always enough enthusiastic pupils at school. They are interested in any undertakings. If the teacher can successfully 'infect' them with his/her idea, it leads to even better outcomes. Of course, the facilitator needs to create a friendly atmosphere, while being current, punchy and creative and try to come up with an original task that has not yet been done. Before setting the creative task, the teacher should try to plan for potential successes and failures. The task of the pupils is to collect as much purposeful information as possible in the framework of the selected topics. The learning goals and objectives should be clear from the outset. Sometimes, at the end of the pupils' first project draft, they raise more questions than answers. I believe this is for the best as it gives the pupils an incentive not to stop there.

The pupils in my class were very interested in the flu virus. We conducted a survey among pupils, teachers, and casual passers-by on the street. During the interviews, it was determined that although "everyone has heard of the flu", few people know how to identify and treat it. We investigated the problem - a doctor agreed to give an explanatory conversation, we filmed everything on a video camera and presented the project to school pupils. During the presentation of the project, the pupils enjoyed watching the interview with the doctor, looked at each other and smiled at seeing themselves and the teachers answering the questions of the reporters in the video, and then actively answering the quiz questions. Pupils received rewards for their efforts.

Reflections

The 21st century is characterised by advanced computer technology. A modern child living in a rapidly developing information space, requires education to implement an approach in which the teacher's main task is not to transmit ready-made conclusions to the pupils, but to help form the pupil's personality through teaching methods and solutions to problems. This approach helps the pupil:

- Disclose and develop their creative and intellectual abilities;

- Avoid the stresses that are common to traditional education, from misconceptions, to anxiety from the need to memorise and cram the material;

- Prepare for mobility and uncertainty, which is extremely important in modern conditions.

My practical work experience confirms the effectiveness of the proposed elements of teaching for developing the research skills of pupils. I have found that it interests pupils and develops their ability to present the results of projects, they actively participate in them and, as a result, they learn. Most of all, they readily recall these pleasant moments outside the walls of the school.

In 2019, I took part in the international project the School of Empathy. I exchanged my professional experiences with Lithuanian colleagues. I discovered they have more developed media technologies. In Ukraine, however, great efforts are required to develop media technologies. Ukrainian pupils are interested in this topic. There will always be an amateur photographer at the school while someone will want to try being a reporter. Leadership and planning are crucial throughout the process - the pupils require some instruction and direction from the teacher for this to be done successfully (more so in the beginning of the activity). When such an activity lacks structure, the pupils struggle to complete the task. As a rule, I request pupils to submit their ideas to the teacher before they continue to develop it. I noticed that a common project outcome is that the pupils generate more questions for further consideration than answers, which pleases me. It indicates that learning is a never-ending process.

I am currently developing my knowledge and skills in cloud computing. I would like to become an expert on this to benefit my pupils. My pupils love blogs, posts, and online services. For this reason, we launched a YouTube channel called 'The Young Biologists' at my school. There are all enthusiasts! Our pupils are new to online forms of testing, independent study, flipped learning, and working with computer programmes while studying subjects. I believe that we will make further advancements in education with the help of technologies and, despite all the difficulties faced, our youth will be competitive among peers from other countries.

Chapter 15

Taking Risks: The Transformative Power of Agency

Mark Rasi

After 20 years in leadership and six as a deputy principal, I found myself on the wrong side of a restructure of senior leadership. Finding myself out of a job was a harsh blow professionally and personally.

My circumstances opened the opportunity to engage in further studies. I already possessed a master's degree, but I was looking to gain further qualifications, knowledge, and skills that would assist me in regaining a senior leadership position. After researching several courses and universities, I decided upon a new MBA programme in Educational Leadership being offered at Tampere University of Applied Sciences (TAMK). This programme particularly appealed to me as it was attempting to break the mould of traditional postgraduate programmes.

My previous tertiary education experiences were mainly instructivist-based, where the lecturer transmitted information to the (often passive) students. This knowledge was assessed by a formal exam. What I found unique about this MBA course was its authentic and social constructivist approach to learning. Students were given agency to select the genre, topic, and means of engagement with learning and assessment instruments. In fact, it was the people (teachers and students) who enabled an authentic and social constructivist learning programme to succeed.

Context

TAMK began delivering their MBA in Educational Leadership to students in September 2017. 25 students from around the globe were admitted to the programme. All students attended the first of three intensive weeks in Tampere, Finland at the beginning of the course. During this intensive week we were introduced to a learning environment that was committed to participatory pedagogy, social constructivism and authentic learning.

The course coordinators, Paivi Mayor and Mark Curcher, challenged and inspired us to be active participants in the programme. They explained to us that they would not take on the mantle of experts or a traditional position of author-itative knowledge. We all came into the course with a wide range of professional backgrounds, experiences, national-ities and education. Therefore, in recognition of this diver-sity and experience in the cohort, the course coordinators explained how a social constructivist learning environ-ment would be more effective in meeting individual learn-ing needs by drawing upon and validating the rich depth of our knowledge and experience.

Because we were an international cohort of students living abroad, a blended learning approach was adopted. Learning experiences were delivered through a regular mix of web-based technologies and supported by the three intensive weeks. The intensive weeks enabled us to develop professional and social connections with each other. These connections provided a stronger 'glue' to bond students and staff as we engaged in the online learning experiences throughout the programme.

Course design

While the MBA programme was structured around traditional business, education, and leadership subjects, there was an intent from the beginning to support an inter-disciplinary approach. This was evident in the first intensive week when the facilitators from different subjects would attend (and contribute) to the introductory presentations for each subject. As students worked through the courses, we were encouraged to draw upon examples and knowledge from other subjects as we found appropriate. The connections that we made were intended to be natural rather than contrived.

Interestingly, there was a greater emphasis on a cross-pollination of ideas when subjects were being studied in the same semester. It was clear that the lecturers were working together to support this process. The responsibility for making connections with current or previous subjects should not solely rest with the lecturers when a social constructivist approach is being taken. Therefore, it is the responsibility of the students to help each other make these connections. No one can make all the connections themselves. During our regular video meetups, different members of the group would identify different connections from time to time.

The good news about delivering a powerful and transformative educational experience is that it can be achieved even with the constraints of traditional course structures. This is because authentic and constructivist pedagogies are not limited by traditional course outcomes. Authentic and constructivist pedagogies are an alternative way of 'getting there'. The bonus is the additional learning outcomes that can occur which are explained further.

People

Students selected for the programme were working in schools, universities, NGOs and the business sector. They were based in Australia, Finland, Holland, Ireland, Japan, Thailand, UAE, UK and USA. The diverse mix maximised the effectiveness of the social constructivist approach to learning. It was impossible for any student not to learn something new from the collective contributions of the group, regardless of their level of education and experience.

The students supported each other in their learning during weekly video conferencing sessions in the first semester of study. As the course progressed beyond the first semester, students transferred from mandatory meetings to self-determined meetings as they saw fit. The course coordinators allocated to themselves tutoring roles so that they could be a point of call at any time and for any subject. They sought to provide students with more support than that of a traditional online teacher.

Pedagogy

The facilitators emphasised how the learning experiences of the students would be shaped by the commitment and contributions of the students to engage in social constructivist pedagogies. The cohort had a varied understanding and experience with this approach to learning and so the course coordinators spent time in the first intensive week to provide their explanation for the benefits of networked learning and knowledge construction.

A course based on social constructivist and networked learning ideas naturally had many group learning experiences, homework, and assessment tasks. Every lecturer and subject required the students to learn and submit work in groups. The cohort was split into three formal study groups of eight or nine students in the first semester to develop close connections with each other and the course materials. My study group of eight met each Saturday to provide support for each other as we attempted to navigate the Learning Management System (LMS) and course requirements. Frequently, we would need to submit the minutes of our discussions to our lecturers for accountability and feedback purposes. Discussions were conducted in various ways including face-to-face, through email, on social media platforms, and using video conferencing technologies.

Personalisation

For me, the two main experiences of personalisation were in the way the learning and assessment tasks were designed and how the tutors practiced their pedagogy of care. Learning and assessment tasks were always designed to enable authentic e-learning to take place.[28] Tasks were always related to the workplace. Often a product was produced that could be used in some way. Some of these promoted the leadership profile of the student when blog posts or LinkedIn articles were published. Other tasks had a practical application in the workplace. These practical applications ranged from financial evaluations and project developments to strategic planning, etc.

The second way that the learning experience was personalised was how the lecturers and tutors responded to my blog posts and LinkedIn articles. I was pointed into directions and towards educational thinkers that they thought I might be interested in. They selected these by observing trends and comments in both my articles and in the emails I sent to them as I reflected on the course and course work. It was this personalisation of instruction that introduced me to other areas of study. The three most significant were rhizomatic learning, phenomenological research, and pedagogy of care. All three consider learning to be more than a linear series of educational interventions imposed upon helpless recipients.

Rhizomatic learning views the learning process much like the creeping roots and shoots of a rhizome. Gilles Deleuze and Felix Guattari first developed this concept, suggesting that the learning process is an unpredictable network of ideas, connections, and knowledge. Phenomenological research aims to transform the lived experience of a subject or subjects into a textual description of the phenomenon. Phenomenological research is effective in helping to understand a subjective experience, gaining insights into motivations and actions, and moving beyond assumptions, conventional wisdom, and scientific positivism. The pedagogy of care considers caring relations as the foundation for pedagogical activity.

These educational positions had a significant impact on how I experienced my studies from that way onwards and the lens that I began to view my education in general.

Breaking out of my comfort zone

The course presented me with transformational opportunities that pushed me out of my comfort zone. The course structure gave me the freedom to explore and construct. I saw a need to provide postgraduate students the opportunity to engage in self-directed and self-determined studies. Due to my experiences on the course, I recognised the importance (and joy) of engaging in self-directed and self-determined learning. I came to believe that universities should be more cognisant of the diverse needs of postgraduate students and that higher education should allow them to develop the capacities and pursue interests that are relevant to them in their personal learning journey. This led to me formulating and submitting a new course proposal to the university which consisted of a course description, learning outcomes, and course contents. I was humbled when I was informed by the university that my ideas and insights were the stimulus for the new Advanced Topics in Educational Leadership course.

The confidence I gained from submitting my course proposal and from the encouragement I received motivated me to submit abstracts to the Association for the Advancement of Computing in Education (AACE) EdMedia conference. My first attempt to submit an abstract was a disaster. I was awake until 4am trying to meet the noon deadline in the United States. While working through the night on my abstract, I was in constant communication with a fellow student and my lecturer. Their advice was very helpful, but it also made me feel inadequate. I was having great difficulty clarifying my ideas and adhering to the style guide. My first submission concerning robotics was rejected.

178

I was relieved that my robotics submission was rejected as it was not what I was passionate about. However, I was enthusiastic about my next submission and the group submission. I was passionate about the experience of postgraduate learners in tertiary studies. This was because I had experienced what it is like to be in an authentic, constructivist learning environment. While my experience had been very satisfying, I had observed that for others it had sometimes been quite frustrating. I was interested to see whether I could resolve this issue for them and the faculty at TAMK. The two papers I was involved in for the conference were connected. The group paper was a collaborative autoethnography that explored the experiences of two students in the educational leadership course. My own paper was a response to that paper. It provided solutions to improving the teacher/student relationship in adult learning contexts.

Designing the poster for the conference was more difficult and satisfying that I had anticipated. I had never designed a poster for such an audience. I discovered that my digital and creativity skills were lacking. I also lacked the software to create a professional product. I had arranged to have my brother print my poster as he is a professional printer and sign writer. It had not occurred to me that he might also be able to help me design my poster. When I mentioned my dilemma to him, he offered to help me. This turned out to be a very powerful experience. During the few hours we worked on the poster, we engaged in many discussions regarding education, skills, technology, communication, etc. It was powerful because my brother did not finish high school. Despite his lack of formal education, he was the expert and it gave me a lot to reflect upon. It was also a significant moment for him as he was able to be the teacher to his older brother. I was very pleased with the final product.

I later presented the collaborative paper in a session with my colleagues at the AACE EdMedia conference in Amsterdam. I also presented my solo work in the poster session. While the conference was the focus of the project, I realised that the preparation provided a more significant learning experience.

Reflections

Whilst the MEL programme implemented innovative and flexible pedagogies, it was still constrained by some traditional approaches to curriculum design; a linear curriculum and learning outcomes developed without a clear understanding of the interests, knowledge, skills or experiences of the cohort. The experiences and expectations of my peer group with the curriculum and teaching methods were mixed. I believe that no single approach to teaching and learning is the best. Teachers need to be comfortable with the approach, skills, and technology they are trying to use, however, this alone is not enough as students need to understand the purpose and rationale behind the subject matter, assessment, and adopted pedagogies.

The experiences surrounding the conference were incredibly powerful. Reflecting on my experiences, I understood that learning is never finished and that a lesson that was taught will not be the final say on any matter. An outcome of my solo project inspired further research on the concepts I explored at the conference to inform the practice of the faculty at TAMK in the MBA programme.

As I reflect on how agency, authenticity, and social constructivism enhanced my learning experiences in the course, I discovered it was not for the reasons that are typically used to justify these approaches. Agency, authenticity, and social constructivism are promoted as being powerful pedagogical approaches that "enhance learning". While this may be the case, I found that the impact on my own emotional wellbeing and personal development were far more profound. Emotional wellbeing and personal development might be an added bonus of tertiary studies, but I would argue that these are far more important than the knowledge and skills that underpin the learning objectives of course outlines in virtually every tertiary subject and programme. Emotional wellbeing and personal stability are the foundations that support all that we do.

What I experienced in the course were rich learning experiences that produced unanticipated professional and personal development outcomes – most of which I had not even considered at the start of the programme. The journey I experienced would not have occurred had I been engaged in a traditional instructivist programme.

Chapter 16

Motivating Students to Solve Community Problems

Girish Nair

I set up Curiosity Gym about four and a half years ago in 2015. I am a mechanical engineer and I worked in the US for 15 years after completing a master's in robotics. I was an automation technologist in several Silicon Valley companies. I returned to India 15 years ago and was the CEO of a mobile and email technology platform company. After having worked in this area for 25 years, I suddenly had the urge to do something completely different. Being a parent of two children, I thought, what about making learning interesting? I thought about it for a year and then finally set up the Curiosity Gym initially as a makerspace.

We create what we call 'innovation hubs' in leading schools and colleges in Mumbai as co-curricular and extra-curricular activities. Topics covered in the innovation hubs include DIY STEAM-based making, design thinking, 3D printing, rapid prototyping, woodworking, programming, robotics and automation for the internet of things' ecosystem of smart devices. Curiosity Gym integrates these hands-on, experiential learning activities with critical thinking. We now work with 12 schools and a college. Most of our school activities work with students from the fourth grade upwards. In India, there is little making in the national curriculum. We run our programme sometimes as a co-curricular activity or as an extracurricular after-school activity. We prefer being co-curricular so that all the children in the school are exposed to making. Overall, the programme is very successful.

We cater to a wide age group. We have other programmes like innovation, entrepreneurship, and design, where we mentor students from higher grades. We also run a full-fledged design thinking hub at a leading management college. Many of the students in college have about five to seven years of work experience when they come back for their MBA. We help these students realise minimum viable prototypes of their ideas that they then submit for business plan contests. The innovation hubs/design thinking hubs are like fablabs and makerspaces and perhaps a little broader in scope - as we are not only thinking about making, we are also thinking about how to inculcate curiosity in children, youth, seniors and entrepreneurs.

We conduct many different types of student-led activities. One project that a few of my colleagues built was an Arduino shield that we called IDIOTWARE, which is an IoT board using hardware and software. We began with the question; how do you make IoT simple using an Arduino board with several sensors and activators? We came up with ideas and designs and later crowdfunded that product. The reason we developed the product was because we were trying to teach Arduino programming in schools and students struggling with the wiring - and we asked, what is a better way that they can get to the story they are trying to build easier and still learn some of the wiring? We designed a product that we created and shared on a crowdfunding platform. The basic goal was to inculcate creativity and innovation in our students so that they can easily transform their IoT-based ideas into viable prototypes.

For example, a team of 11th grader girls in one of our schools had an issue with sanitary napkins not being easily available to them in their school. As part of the 30-week course they made a sanitary napkin dispenser - which went through three prototypes - the final version of which they installed in their school. The students were exposed to computer aided design (CAD) and 3D printing, material selection, and learnt Arduino programming to control a motor based on light sensing. The team broke up into the prototype implementers and a sub team focused on the collateral and crowdfunded campaign - which eventually raised enough to fund dispensers in 13 different municipal schools in the area.

The boys in the same class did something completely different. They made a 3D printed object to prevent their football laces coming undone. Other teams worked on diverse projects such as a wardrobe organiser, or a call button for an intoxicated customer to call a cab from a bar.

Curiosity Gym also offers workshops on machine learning, AI, Arduino, Raspberry Pi, robotics, data visualisation, electronics, IoT, and other hobby classes like origami as well, at their makerspace in Mumbai, India. For individual students, Curiosity Gym even offers individual one-on-one technology mentorships and internships. Students can build a socially relevant project or robots for various competitions, work on submissions for international contests like Google Science Fair, etc. Mentees of Curiosity Gym have acquired making and design skills and honed their ability to imagine questions not traditionally asked in their school curriculum - and have since been admitted to some of the best colleges in the world.

Besides running innovation hubs, which are experiential learning/tinkering labs where students can make and be mentored on projects, Curiosity Gym has an applied learning programme on sciences and social sciences that it offers at schools. This programme maps the curriculum to a simulated/real world environment, so that students can appreciate why they are learning what they do. Activities in some of the sessions include:

- Converting one's mobile to a microscope to look at a mosquito's leg;

- Measuring the diameter of a human hair using the principle of physics, a laser and a normal ruler;

- 3D printing a complex gear;

- Creating math puzzles using concepts of binary; and

- Making a self-balancing robot.

Initially, the mentors start by making sure that the students are enthused about the problem that they pick to solve, by ensuring they can articulate the problem, state why it is relevant, and plan the steps around how it can be resolved. They are encouraged to ask stakeholders what the issue is, finding out about different perspectives, debating different solutions, and working as a team. They are encouraged to not shoot down other people's ideas and try and get the best features of many of the proposed solutions so that an optimised solution can be found. They do rapid prototyping and guide them when needed. They may often get stuck due to not having the skills to use some of the tools, unfamiliarity with electronics, programming, or simply not being mechanically inclined.

Examples of socially relevant or technically challenging projects worked on by Curiosity Gym students include:

- A girls' team making a sanitary napkin dispenser for a school and crowdfunding it to fund the same in several municipal schools in the area.

- Making a power harnessing-broom for the Swachh Bharat initiative (a cleanliness initiative run at the

Government of India level) used to incentivise sweepers so that they can charge their mobiles by converting the kinetic energy of sweeping to harnessed electrical power.

- Making a spectrometer to measure impurities in milk.

- A 3D printed queue manager to manage a set of printers at the hubs.

- An ion thruster prototype.

- A skipping rope that counts skips so that you can share your exercise routine with friends.

- A spoon assist to stabilise a spoon while eating for Parkinson's patients.

- An automated dog food dispenser.

Motivating students to be persistent and not give up after the first few failures is the key role of mentors, especially when the projects are technically challenging. "The satisfaction achieved when one is able to conquer a problem due to trial and error and persistence to reach one's eventual goal is worth the effort" is the constant refrain.

The innovation hub is considered one of the most exciting classes in the school timetable in all the schools in which we operate. Students look forward to coming there because of its interdisciplinary approach. They learn a lot and interact with things and make things. Examples of a couple of interdisciplinary sessions in the innovation hub are:

- A binary card trick to guess someone's birthday from a set of 5 cards. (Hint: $2^5 = 32$). The trick involves linking binary concepts of mathematics and computer science and is told with the historical context of how an ancient war could have been won using the knowledge of binary numbers, centuries before computers were invented.

- Another example of an inter-disciplinary session is designing a game that involves design thinking, cryptography, geography, historical monuments and 3D printing and design.

One challenge in starting hubs in schools is for the school management to understand how important it is to allocate time for activities at the hub in the school timetable. Many educators are open to having this as an after-school activity. As a result, typically less than 5% of the school students opt to stay back and miss the school bus. Addressing parents, parent-teacher associations (PTAs), and school management early in the school's annual timetable planning cycle is essential to overcome this hurdle.

Overall, I am very optimistic that educators worldwide are realising the need for activity, inquiry, and project-based learning and hence this hurdle of allocation of time will be overcome. The overall desired impact of Curiosity Gym is to reach millions of students and adults around the world to be curious and innovative by simplifying concepts and surfacing the interdisciplinary nature of much in life.

Chapter 17

Living History Experiences

Lynn Hannay

I was fortunate enough recently to bump into two young men, brothers, at a party. I had taught them in their primary years, and they were keen to tell me their news and to chat about old times. They wanted to talk about the living history experiences they had taken part in with me, how they remembered them vividly, and the effect they had on shaping their futures. One had just graduated with a degree in ancient history and philosophy ("you brought it all to life! I would never have learned or remembered so much if we had stayed in the classroom") and the other was undertaking a degree in sports therapy. The first is obvious — but a degree in sports therapy linked to living history? He explained that he wants to work with injured and disabled servicemen to help their rehabilitation. He traces his interest in war and its effects on the individual to WWII work in year 6. He explained that the whole project had awoken empathy for his fellow man which was heightened by other experiences in life. Not even I saw that one coming!

The learning activity outline

At the Lyceum school, where I shared the role of headteacher and year 6 teacher with Jeremy Rowe (neither of us wanted to be in the office and were both passionate about teaching), we constructed a totally immersive, thematic, holistic curriculum developed from the needs of the children we worked with. The curriculum took into account the contents of the National Curriculum yet went far beyond to create a broad and balanced curriculum with an emphasis on the arts, considered the whole child, and paid close attention to the developmental stages of each group of children and the individuals within each grouping. We reviewed this annually, with all staff involved, considering any relevant new ideas, trends, and best practice but keeping our focus on the needs of the children in our school. Each year began with guidelines for teachers which we expected to evolve as the year progressed, allowing teachers to use their professional judgement to respond to their class and incorporate the interests of the children along with having the space to respond to global and local events.

The school was founded in 1997 by myself and Jeremy Rowe so we could teach with an emphasis on experiential, child-led, collaborative learning with the performing and visual arts at the centre of school life to develop self-confidence, team work, self-esteem, a sense of unity, and inclusive, positive attitudes. This was our reaction to the marginalisation of the arts and the increase in subject teaching in primary schools. We had many battles with Ofsted over the years but held tight to our ethos and beliefs in how children best learn.

The recruitment of staff to our ethos and vision, which included them buying into Living History, was vital to our success. Teachers either 'got it' or they did not get the job. I recall one teacher coming for a visit and finding herself involved in a WWII meal, fully costumed, with staff and some parents as we prepared for a WWII evacuation experience. She got the job - her reaction was perfect – and she stayed for 15 years.

I include here a description of how an evacuation residential experience might typically look, as an example of living history. There were always changes and adaptations depending on children's prior knowledge and the profile of the group.

The term would begin by children arriving at school to find they had to climb over sandbags and enter through a sacking door into a 1940s classroom with a Morrison shelter and a 1940s sitting room at one end (all staff were expected to change their classrooms termly to engage the children in a new topic). There would be a box of clothes on the floor and WWII research books around so that each child could create their own costume. The start of war speech by Winston Churchill would be played and a discussion would take place to establish what the children already knew and questions they wanted answered. This allowed for planning to be adapted. There would be a few weeks of facilitating learning in class, using the local environments, museums, and visitors. That learning would include the breadth of the curriculum.

Geography: European and world maps, changing borders, diaspora of peoples, reclaiming and rebuilding land, local post war building programmes.

History: A focus on research, historical skills, using primary and secondary evidence — what can we learn about the war from xxxx and how reliable is that information, family history and local/school history.

Religious education: Judaism and the Holocaust.

Music: WWII songs and music/entertainment, how this affected morale, and music tutors and head of music were fully involved.

Art and D/T: War photographers, war artists, Henry Moore and the air-raid shelter sketches, the purpose of art in recording war, knitting, sewing, book making, box construction, observational drawing, using a variety of media, imaginative/creative art, junk modelling, woodwork.

Science: inventions, forces, nutrition.

Maths: coordinates, codes, number patterns, rationing, weight, proportion, scale, imperial measurement.

Dance: jive, creative dance stimulated by fear, parting of families, air raids etc.

Drama: we always wrote a play with the children, appropriate to their particular interests. Once we adapted 'The Elephant in the Garden' by Michael Morpurgo but usually we wrote from scratch. One year we put on an ENSA performance with a particularly musical and theatrical group, another we re-enacted a BBC broadcast, another took place in the underground air-raid shelter and had Vera Lynn visit to sing and Henry Moore to draw. Once performance grew out of a group of children who wanted to commemorate family who had died and was based around letters they wrote to these ancestors. These plays were driven by the children, costumed by them, they created staging, lighting effects and worked together to be stagehands, performers, prompts etc.

English: All children read novels set in WWII to enhance learning. These included books about the lives of children in other parts of the world so they gained a global perspective. Creative writing, factual writing, and other genres were used to record

aspects of the project and the retrieval of information from a variety of sources was key. Presentations and drama developed oral skills. In addition, all children physically made a book in which to display their work. These books needed to be made by two children and there was lots of support for each other in creating a beautifully displayed book.

PSHE: we did a lot of talking, discussing, and debating around issues that arose. It was vital to ensure this could happen daily when doing an intense project about an emotive subject.

Using technology: we had laptops and iPads available for use by the children for additional research and, crucially, to allow them to record and present their work in a variety of formats — written, video, photographic slideshows, sharing to YouTube, creating mobile apps and websites etc. Technology was embedded in all our projects and used to support the curriculum.

We began to do family research early in the project. It was essential to meet with parents and to get them to support their children and to ensure that if sensitive issues arose, we could be alerted and would agree how they were to be dealt with. This was very pertinent one year when we discovered we had in the same class a child whose grandfather had been in the Hitler Youth, a child whose family had all but been wiped out in concentration camps, and a child related to Oswald Moseley!

We supported family research carefully; setting tasks and targets with individuals and working closely with parents. This culminated in children creating a printed or online family history book. We had children who told us their families were not involved in the war i.e. no one fought; but we often had some interesting outcomes from these children, as everyone had families around at the time and their research brought balance including Home Front discoveries, and a non-Eurocentric world view. All children were encouraged to research the events behind initial discoveries e.g. "my great- grandfather was a Beven boy" or "my grandmother was in the First Aid Nursing Yeomanry (FANY)" or "my family lived in India so what was a Beven boy? "the FANY?" and "what was happening in India at the time?"

As we approached the time for the living history experience, we talked about evacuation and made gas mask boxes, ration cards, name tags, and lists of things to take. We met at the railway station under a sign saying, 'Evacuees gather here' and waved good-bye to anxious parents as we boarded the train with duffle bags, brown paper packages, teddy bears, and sandwiches in greaseproof paper. We were met by the warden of the residential accommodation dressed in 1940s clothing and escorted to our accommodation on a farm. By now everyone was fully involved in their character and as head of the evacuating school I engaged the matron to do nit and teeth inspection before allocating beds and organising activities.

Over the next few days we worked the land, dug in potatoes, picked vegetables, fed chickens and collected eggs, mucked out pigs, and moved logs for the farmer. Children helped make Lord Woolton's pie along with parsnip pudding and other wartime delicacies and those brave enough to do so skinned rabbits and plucked pigeons — I was amazed at how many volunteered. How to feed ourselves was a big source of conversation and the children learned how lucky they were to be on a farm. Our lovely ex-secretary, who had been an evacuee herself, came along to show the children a week's rations and help them plan menus.

There were 1940s style school daily and visitors like home guards, land girls, and Italian internees as well as Winston Churchill. The children interviewed and drew or photographed them using an old Box Brownie. In the evenings, we knitted scarves and socks for servicemen, sewed on buttons, darned socks, and wrote letters home.

Just when everything was feeling cosy, we staged an air raid. The staff had previously made a spitfire out of boxes which we put out into a field and once the all clear sounded the children emerged from under tables to see it on fire in the distance. During the air raid, teachers kept spirits up by singing whilst others created the relevant sounds around us.

We approached the wreckage with the children (health and safety paramount here) and discussed what we could see and what had happened. Gradually, the children collected the airman's belongings which were strewn around the field. His boots, kitbag, wallet, photos, papers, ration book, identity card, headphones, magazine, etc.

Back inside, we worked together to build a profile of the pilot and wrote a report to send to the authorities. The children were totally committed to helping discover who this pilot was and to ensure his family received the news. They were being historians, piecing together evidence, so much so that when a newspaper reporter arrived asking questions, they closed ranks without a word from us.

Back at school, children chose to record their experience in a variety of ways; most often in pairs or small groups. This led to an assembly for parents and the rest of the school, which included reading written contributions, showing video footage or photos, short drama sketches etc.

Why I tried this approach and what I considered whilst designing it

"We all have roots in the past. Our families extend back into it; houses, streets and towns were shaped by it; and it made possible all aspects of our daily lives. Yet those who inhabited it often elude our understanding. Living history brings them closer to us by recreating the practical details of their lives - what they wore, ate and lived in; how they fought, farmed or worked in new industrial towns."[29]

Children taking part in living history is something about which I have been passionate for most of my teaching career. I am sure some onlookers see it as a bit of fun and a lark - dressing up, but for me it is a fundamental part of how children can best learn about history. The former education secretary, Michael Gove, would have us believe that learning about history is purely the acquisition of facts in a chronological order, but there is so much more to history education than that; the acquisition of the historical skills of enquiry and questioning, the use of evidence (both primary and secondary), sequencing, and the vital connections to be made with other curricular areas. As they grow, children need to be able to put the historical era they are studying in context to make those connections and comparisons. It is important to ensure that children develop an interest into not only learning about the history of the country in which they live but also that of the wider world, develop their sense of enquiry so that they broaden their minds and gain a sense of the past, and understand how the lives we live now are still rooted in it and what it can inform our future. To achieve these aims, teachers need to engage children with history they can touch and identify with, bring it to life, and provide access to real artefacts and simulated situations. This is why undertaking work on Vikings, Romans, Victorians, WWII and Tudors is successful with primary children in the UK as there are places to visit and quality artefacts available to stimulate discussion and the imagination - elements of the political, religious, and social situations are within their understanding and there are important connections with the histories of other countries.

There is a need for teachers of young children to find ways to engage them with the past, paying attention to how they learn and their stage of development. That means finding real ways to stimulate their minds and excite them. If we gain their interest and excitement as primary pupils, they will go on to want to learn more at the secondary stage and retain that interest into later life. This is apparent from the number of pupils I have taught who have gone on to study history at GCSE, A-level, and at university; and who, when I meet them, like the brothers mentioned above, want to talk about the experiences the school provided for them.

Living history is an extension of my commitment to experiential and child-centred learning. I am reminded of the old Chinese proverb attributed to Confucius, "Tell me, I'll forget. Show me, I'll remember. Involve me, I'll understand". Benjamin Franklin is said to have reworked this proverb in this way - "Tell me and I forget, teach me and I may remember, involve me and I learn". There are other versions, but the message is crystal clear. If we want children to understand, learn and retain information, concepts, and skills, there needs to be activity and involvement. Take children either metaphorically or physically somewhere historical, and let them live the history, and they will remember, learn, and understand.

I have been very fortunate to have spent my entire teaching career in London which has so many historical sites close to hand where it is possible to engage children and support them to make the necessary connections to extend their learning. Many of our greatest monuments and sites both in London and across Great Britain now provide some living history experiences, for example, guides that dress authentically and stay in character while showing groups around. A stage on from this type of living history is a place like Kentwell Hall,[30] which provides full and extensive re-enactments of specific historical events.

Specific historical events are difficult for schools to re-enact for children. My focus has always been on giving them a feel for the domestic life of a given era, how real people (especially children) lived. I have done this in the knowledge that we cannot be absolutely sure of the experience of those who lived in Tudor or Victorian Britain - what we can offer is our interpretation of those experiences based on our reading of the interpretation of historians - and who knows how far from the truth that takes us.

Jay Anderson, founder of the Association for Living History, Farm and Agricultural Museums (ALFHAM),[31] which offers support and advice on historical skills, says that critics who claim living history is misleading are missing the point because while history itself cannot change, our interpretation of the past is constantly changing and those involved in living history can respond to those changes. The mission statement of ALFHAM is to share practical knowledge and skills amongst those who make history relevant to contemporary lives. Their website says, "Living history means different things to different people".

Jay Anderson identified three groups of living historians in his work, 'Time-machines: The world of living history':[32]

1. Those who interpret how people lived.

2. Those who use living history as a research tool to test theories and explore material culture.

3. Those labelled 'history buffs' who create personas for themselves based on a person or a blend of persons.

At the Lyceum school, we developed a mixture of all three. I believe we gave children a real feeling for an era whilst being pragmatic about the compromises we made for the sake of practicality and health and safety.

Another reason to use living history, along with other types of residential and whole day experiences, was to provide powerful professional development for staff. We always involved new staff in these events regardless of which age group they taught, as I believe this involvement taught them more about our commitment to concrete experience, our views on how children learn and our values, vision and ethos than any other single thing.

What I observed as I tried this approach and what results came from it

As with any form of learning where children are actively involved, collaboration happens and learning is rapid, enhanced, and retained. Motivation is high and children encourage and support each other to do better through their enjoyment of learning. Children take control of their learning and level of involvement. Progress is particularly noticeable in less able or less confident children. Take them out of the stress of a formal classroom and they do not even notice they are learning at times. They all move forward.

The learning takes place academically and the motivation to write or record in some way becomes urgent because there is something real to say, even for children normally reluctant to put pen to paper. Ideas flow more easily. The emotional and social learning and development is striking. New friendships are made, children show skills and strengths and weaknesses that were not apparent in a classroom, and staff see children in a different light. The shared experiences return to the classroom and remain a powerful anchor point to be referred to in the future. Shared experiences are bonding. The children were able and willing to suspend disbelief and to go along with any scenario. On one occasion we emerged from an air-raid shelter and a plane was flying over. A boy who normally cynical waved and shouted, "It is a Spitfire - one of ours!" And it was! Total coincidence.

But do not take my word for it. This is what children who filled in evaluative questionnaires think of living history:

"I learned I am good at working in teams and cooperating with other people. I can plan things ahead and remember things well."

"I was surprised that I could be responsible and look after my own possessions and my special clothes."

"I can work in a group and communicate and I am good at helping people."

"I learned that I need to be quick and efficient and not do things the long way around. I learned to try things before I decide they are hard or easy, I learned to rely on myself and to trust myself. I also learned not to judge and look down on other eras."

"I learned I could cope without my parents and be independent."

"I learned to make connections with modern life."

"I could have got it from a book and read it, but I experienced it and understood it and now I have my own opinion. It helped me remember better."

"In a book you use sight but on a trip, you use all your senses."

"A book is someone else's opinion but going on a trip you learn for yourself and make your own mind up."

"Lots of the things we learned about everyday life you cannot learn from a book."

"It is much more exciting. When you read about history you cannot emotionally connect."

"We learned to do things instead of reading about them."

"In that week I learned so many things, most of them unreachable if we had stayed in class and read."

"When you experience something, you understand it better."

"The experience changes the way you look at things and think about them."

For the teachers taking part, the experiences led to new ideas - not just living history but other immersive projects to motivate and spark children's interests. One New Zealand teacher sent me photographs of him recreating the landing of Europeans on New Zealand soil with his class. He had convinced his school in New Zealand of the value of living history.

Tips for facilitators

If I was advising a teacher who was interested in enabling a living history experience for their class, I would say start simply. The first time I did this, I created a Victorian classroom for one morning in school. Children were given flat caps (borrowed or from the charity shop) or mop caps (made from old sheets) and were given Victorian style lessons. The year before I took a class to the Ragged School in Bethnal Green to watch this in action. The following occasion, I organised a whole day and involved other adults in the activities and began to gather more costumes from charity shops and people willing to help with sewing.

Get help from parents in creating costumes. WWII are the easiest to pull together but with families onboard someone will sew pinafores or cut down jackets for Victorians.

Plan appropriate activities. They did not have to be grand - just of the era. Remember, you are giving the children a feel for what life was like. Cooking is always a winner.

Start from the children's own knowledge and what they want to find out. Make it collaborative using any expertise amongst staff and parents but also enlist their help.

Make sure your own knowledge is correct and thoroughly researched as this will give you confidence and the ability to guide the children and other staff. I used to prepare character reading packs for new participants, especially as we were a group with wide-ranging cultural and ethnic backgrounds. This enriched the experience and allowed new ideas to be contributed.

Never be afraid to admit to children that you did not know something. This gives a chance for them to really contribute and for you to research together. Equally, be prepared to let the children lead at times and to adapt plans accordingly.

If the senior leadership in the school or parents are doubters as to the value of the activity, be ready to show the progress made by the children and to document this as well as the attainment in a range of subjects. Get the children to complete evaluation questionnaires.

Teachers need to be fully committed, dressed appropriately, do their own research and stay in their given character/role as much as possible, and they should clearly explain to the children when and why they come out of character. Being aware of the level of child involvement and knowledge helps teachers to guide and monitor their own behaviour. We tried not to be flippant or make amusing comments to each other from an adult standpoint so as not to detract from the experience for the child - despite some hilarious moments.

Whatever experience is offered to children, try to make sure they are costumed and fully involved. These experiences at the Lyceum were anything from an Egyptian market recreated in the school hall for a day where children in character engaged with their visiting parents using hot seating or serving food, or a Victorian country weekend to four nights living in a Tudor barn, eating Tudor style menus from wooden platters and doing a walking tour of Lavenham (Suffolk) in full costume!

Steven Hales' essay, 'The primary school experience'[33] ends with this: "My class debated the issue of which was more important, books or living history, and resolved that both play an important part in the teaching and learning of history. One of the children said that living history gives you 'A real picture in your head', while another said that books give you information against which you can check out your own ideas. One of the children mentioned that information from books can be biased, and that a living history production enables you to 'make your own judgments'".

Melissa Thibault has published an article called 'Bring history to life with a living history day!'[34] She states that building skills, assessing the importance of individuals in living history, constructing a historical narrative, and formulating historical questions are important when challenging children to think historically. She maintains that those skills should be nurtured from the moment the children are exposed to history and that focusing on an individual in history provides a manageable chunk for small children to work with e.g. Florence Nightingale. She goes on to say that, "The key is to move from reporting facts, an activity that can be done without demonstrating any understanding, to historical inquiry, an activity that engages the student and brings the subject to life". She maintains that living history is the way forward. To present a living history day, she writes, "Students must synthesise the information they learned to create an exhibit representative of their subject; this cannot happen unless they are actually engaged in the event". This is what the Lyceum children did when they created their Egyptian market. They did the research, which enabled them to present their day with authority.

In terms of what can be offered to children as living history experiences, there are several variations:

1. Invite in a historical character to talk to the children and be interviewed. There are companies like the Fresh Water Theatre Company[35] who do this very well or a member of staff can take on a role. These types of interactive workshops are useful if it is not possible to plan an educational experience outside of school.

2. Use members of staff and/or the children themselves to take part in 'hot-seating'. We often used the idea during WWII residential experiences where children were able to interview Winston Churchill, a member of the WAAF, and an Italian internee (all willing staff members).

3. Use a freeze-frame technique in costume to recreate a specific event. This requires a great deal of research prior to enable the creation of a tableau.

4. Visit historical sites where they provide characters in costume who meet and greet the children and guide them.

5. Visit historical sites where they provide re-enactments of specific historical events.

6. A re-enactment day in school e.g. the creation of an Egyptian market where other children visit and interview the presenting children in character.

7. A residential experience immersing the children in the lifestyle of a specific era e.g. a Victorian country weekend.

In the context of school life, it is important that:

- The children are fully involved and encouraged so they are immersed in the experience.

- Parents are engaged to support their children.

- Teachers plan what they want children to learn during the experience. It should not be merely reinforcing what has been learned previously. That preparation work should lead up to the visit or experience, but that teachers should be aware that the experience itself should stand on its own in the case of a living history residential/day trip and not be made invalid because of too much prior teaching.

- When planning a history topic, teachers think well in advance about which aspects of knowledge and skills can be best taught through living history i.e. it should not be merely an add-on.

- Follow-up work should be sufficiently focused, engaging and appropriate.

- Written records of the event should be carefully thought through, i.e. a diary is not always the best form of recording and maybe nothing at all needs recording in writing by individual children.

- The experience should not be trivialised or compromised by inaccurate information or presentations, e.g. be clear what the music is for the era, so do not present Oliver as being Victorian.

"Facts, dates, lists of Kings and Queens - all tell some of the story of our past. But there is nothing like re-enacting the reality to bring it all vividly to life"- this is taken from 'Living in the Past, an English Heritage publication.

Through living history, our children reach back to touch their roots in the past. Their experiences are full of meaning to them and that is why they learn. A word from a re-enactor: "You live and breathe the past at a re-enactment: it is all around you, in everything you see, hear and smell. Somehow it seems much more real than the present day".[36]

Chapter 18

Constructionist Modification of the NASA Touchdown Lander Lesson

Nick Giacobbe and Brandon Rodriguez

This story serves as a good example of how a constructionist approach can be applied to an existing lesson to heighten the student experience. To be clear, we believe that this method is activity agnostic and could be applied widely to different activities in different disciplines. In this instance, it was the perfect fit between a school culture, an adaptable lesson, and the learning theory. Let's begin with the setting.

Our first implementation of this was work was at Burley School, a pre-k to 8 public, neighbourhood school in the Lakeview neighbourhood of Chicago. For those not acquainted with Lakeview, I could see the lights at Wrigley Field from my classroom window. Burley is a literature, writing, and technology magnet school and they emphasise using student inquiry as the basis for their curriculum. It is the feeling of the faculty there that it is important for students to have personal investment in their work and much of what they learn stems from their own investigations based on their personal wonderings.

214

Something taken very seriously at Burley, is the design of classroom settings and how classroom cultures are set up. While there are many ways that teachers there use technology to take learning opportunities to the next level, the first order of the day is making sure that the environment is such that students feel intellectually safe and empowered to take intellectual risks.

Constructionism, as a learning philosophy, meshes well with the kind of work happening in places like Burley. Constructionism is all about conversations and great ideas spreading amongst groups of passionate learners. One notion of Seymour Papert that is embodied here is 'hard fun'. Papert described this as deep engagement with creating. He saw that learners did not want things that are easy, rather they want to do things that challenge them, that matter to them personally. He eschewed the notion that we need to sugar-coat or gamify things to make them more palatable.

The final piece is the lesson provided by NASA JPL's education team. This lesson is called 'Touchdown'.[37] The context is that pupils are going to experience the design challenges that NASA faces in creating solutions for landing a passenger craft safely on the moon. In this endeavour, they will work in small teams to create a shock absorbing craft out of paper cups, index cards, rubber bands, marshmallows, tape and plastic straws. The astronauts, represented by two large marshmallows, must handle the shock of landing in their student-built lander.

Why I tried it and what were my design considerations

For this project, we talked through the lesson as designed and decided to make a few adjustments. Our process revolved around throwing ideas into a Google doc and letting the ideas marinate. We spent quite some time rethinking many aspects of the lesson and determining how we could adjust it so that students could get the most out of the experience.

Our first change was in the duration of the activity. We shifted from a single class period to three class periods each containing a single design cycle. Our thought was that if you only have one design, it feels very summative and limits your ability to adjust, learn from others, and ideate. With the activity spanning three days, it allowed students to create multiple artefacts (landers, blueprints, vlogs) and incorporate peer-to-peer feedback, which is what constructionism is all about.

The big burning question here for educators is how to document and assess all this student work. In this instance, we used Seesaw, an online portfolio app.[38] It allowed students to create media (pictures, narrated pictures, videos) that highlighted their process, both successes and struggles. In this way, the students and teacher were able to see the prior knowledge of a team going into a design, their thinking in-process as they design, their inspirations, and how they felt it turned out in the end.

216

The other piece that we included was Mitch Resnick's creative learning spiral.[39] Resnick was a pupil of Papert's and is now the head of the lab that Papert started at the Media Lab, the Lifelong Kindergarten group. Resnick sees creative learning as a spiral where students imagine an idea, create it, play around with it, share it with their peers, and then reflect on the experience. Then, they reimagine their work and the cycle continues.

On day one, the lesson was introduced, and they received the context for the challenge followed by imagine, create, play, and share. On the second and third days, students would start the day reflecting on what they and their peers had created. In this way, we primed the room for innovation through involving the learners in careful analysis of their work and that of their classmates. After reflection, they followed the spiral through the share phase.

It should be mentioned that our introduction, where we set the context, was also adjusted. In the original lesson design, there was quite a bit of frontloading. We wanted to provide a more open, sandbox scenario for our learners so that they would have more opportunity to make mistakes, play around, and discover solutions for themselves. In our model, we gave the background for the challenge and laid out ground rules for using the materials.

In the imagine stage, each student team would imagine their ideal lander and then draw it as a blueprint. As a management technique, teams were required to draw their blueprint, photograph it, upload it to the class portfolio, and then show it to us before they could access the supply table. This created a natural bottleneck and prevented a mass rush on the supply table. This also freed us up to aid them with any difficulty the students would have with using the technology while also establishing an important routine. To move forward, students needed to document their process. By establishing this routine at the front end, it became a natural step in the students' workflow for the project.

In the create stage, students would gather materials from the supply table and begin constructing their landers. As facilitators, we were very careful to document this process and not directly intervene. It was very important to encourage the autonomy of the students and ensure that they felt like this was an open opportunity. These kinds of open-ended learning experiences are so rare and foreign to some students that it is truly a precious thing that needs to be guarded.

A helpful note here is that as we documented the process, we made sure to pay special care to observing the photos of students working in this phase. We studied their hands. As students build and collaborate, how they manipulate the materials, and who is holding the materials tells a story unto itself. As the students played and tinkered with the supplies, they regularly came up with new ideas that they incorporated into their designs. A way to keep track of these changes and to encourage students to be reflective about their experience was to have them take an image of their completed artefact, in this case a lander, at the end of the phase. Then, they would create an audio track describing how their artefact evolved from what they intended in their blueprint.

For the play and share phases, we had students create slow motion videos of dropping their landers and then sharing those videos on the class Seesaw feed. For the reflection phase, students were encouraged to create a video reflecting on what they had learned from the process and what their plans were moving forward. They also were encouraged to look through the class feed to see if there were potentially inspiring designs there. They could also chime in on the work of other students by asking them questions, providing them with helpful insights, or simply acknowledging their good work. This was a way of pollinating the room with ideas. This phase is how we would end each day and begin the next day. In this way, the beginning and end of each session provided time for thoughtful discernment about what the next steps were and primed them for creative exploration.

The results

To get a real feel for how this went, we review one team: Team Atlantis. Due to the way that students were monitoring and recording their process, we could have done this with any of the teams. The reason we have chosen Team Atlantis is because of their growth over time and their ability to communicate how the process shaped their thinking in the reflection stages.

On day one, they drew a quick sketch outlining what they intended to build. Convinced of the success of their design, they stayed very close to this design throughout the create phase. Their design used tiny marshmallows inside the cup and on the base for cushioning. They also stuck straws through the top to serve as a tool to keep the marshmallows in. Finally, they added a parachute made of aluminium foil. When it was time to test their model for play and share, they dropped it for the first time on camera. They quickly discovered that the weight of their design was not offset by the parachute as it crashed hard onto the floor. This team was led by a student that had done many constructionist experiences before, so she calmly and wisely addressed her teammate. "It is going to be great," she said. "Today is just our first try, so we are just learning. I have already got new ideas to try." On their first try, many students try to perfect. This student, with her prior knowledge of the learning spiral, had faith in the process and in herself. She trusted that she would have more opportunities to improve and that failure was something to learn from, not something to be avoided.

On day two, Team Atlantis began by reflecting on their previous work, shared some feedback for their peers, and drafted a blueprint of the day's design. Their voice note on the blueprint told me what they were keeping and what they were adding to their design. While this is helpful information, the best part is that they also gave their rationale for what they kept and what they left out. This is particularly important because that information cannot be gleaned from the picture alone. They note that the new design features notecards on the bottom to help it to float better. This gives me new information about their thinking, but also leaves me with new questions when their next artefact looks significantly different from the blueprint. Luckily, they left a voice note of their thinking here as well.

During the create and play stage, the team was not satisfied with how the parachute was working but found that the index cards as wings were a major success in slowing down the descent. As a teacher, what I like to hear is how they articulate how and why they are adjusting. What I see here is that they are keeping some design elements from the first model that worked well while trying a new base.

Jumping ahead to day three, I saw a blueprint that reflected design features from the first two days, as well a curious new improvement. They had added a propeller with index card fans at the top. As I listened to their description of how they had designed their blueprint, I heard that they were attributing the idea of the propeller to another team. This was precisely what we wanted to happen. Through the routine sharing of artefacts of their thinking back and forth, they had, in a sense, pollinated the room with their ideas. This is by design and is at the heart of constructionism. The conversations that they had inspired new iterations and designs. It is also worth noting that these students gave attribution where it is due. This tied back into the culture of the classroom. The students understood that their success was communal, and their individual successes stemmed from the contributions they had received and made within that community.

The highlight of the entire process was the final reflection. Team Atlantis' final task was to reflect on their three-day journey with their three landers side-by-side. There was something about seeing those finished artefacts from each day together that drew out new connections and thinking from the team. As they described the first two landers, the student shared a problem they needed to solve, their planned solution, how it turned out, and how that result informed them about what new issues the process had uncovered. The third lander, however, followed a different pattern. As they discussed their process for creating this lander, their thinking was mostly about adaptation. They had discovered what worked and what did not from their earlier trials and the trials of their peers, and then refined their prototype based on that information. Through collaboration, iteration, and synthesis of new information, they had made something truly great. To illustrate the point, the student on camera dropped the lander to highlight how far they had come. As it softly landed, she said, "It is actually the one that works. It does much better than the other ones."

As a student described the final prototype, her smile and excitement highlighted a realisation that she had made. In this moment, she understood what they were able to accomplish was never guaranteed. She was not on a fixed path with a specific, predetermined solution as the target. For this reason, her success felt authentic and earned.

What I would try next time

The modifications made on the NASA Touchdown lesson were shared at several educator workshops in Southern California as part of the Jet Propulsion Laboratory's educator professional development meetings. The student artefacts from the original implementation, along with the smiling students in the video reflections, served as a compelling case for teachers in the community to reproduce this work. Several of these teachers were kind enough to share their stories and detail the conditions in which they implemented this constructionist focus. While the selection of the classroom portfolio app varied from teacher to teacher, in each case, students were tasked to document their blueprint and the lander they constructed to a classroom community site. Primary grade teachers kept the lesson at three days, while one 8th grade teacher elected to do it only two. However, in each instance, the presence of student exchange of ideas using the online platform consistently showed student communication and reflection, both on their own designs and the designs of their peers.

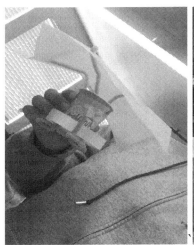

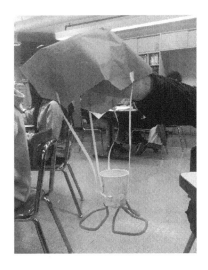

The 8th grade teacher who recreated this work noted that the second day "...was even more important than the first. They had to reflect on the results gathered in the first test and use that as inspiration to revise and build their second lander. Students had to assess the features of the successful landers to evaluate what qualities made them effective". It is important to note that many of us as classroom teachers with a litany of topics to cover may have moved on to the next topic at the end of day one, yet teachers doing this work are quick to note that it is not until day two that the presentation of learning manifests itself fully.

As highlighted above, the crux of the success of these constructionist adaptations must begin with culture. It may take students some time to adjust to the notion that they can (and are encouraged to) fail today, in the hopes of extracting information for their attempts tomorrow. Success is not measured by the ticking down of the clock to end the period. For educators looking to recreate these activities, it is of course clear that not every lab and activity can be extended to three times its original length. However, even picking a few projects that have 'high-spiralling potential' can assist in creating this culture of exploration and hard fun. Open-ended, sandbox-type projects, typically those that rely on the engineering design cycle are good candidates. Regardless of grade level or discipline, the opportunity to work collaboratively and demonstrate their learning though revision makes science engaging and authentic to careers in STEM.

Chapter 19

Achieving Sustainable Transformative Learning: Reflections on Educational Adventures in Kazakhstan

Sue Parkes

'I have never stopped,

the drive for me is to never stop learning'

—Nishit Sharma - traveller and blogger

W hy Kazakhstan? I reflect on my childhood; I spent hours perusing the family Reader's Digest atlas, looking at the Caucasian mountains, and reading our Encyclopaedia Britannica about the culture, the food, the ethnic groups of these areas, never considering that I would be living and working on the steppe.

Move forward a few decades. Here was an opportunity, a little off the well-worn international teaching track. The appeal for me to apply to work inside a post-Soviet country, being able to work within a distinct education system (Nazarbayev Intellectual Schools – NIS)[40] where skilled local and international teachers work collaboratively to facilitate critical thinking in high ability learners selected from the public education system and importantly, team teach the subject Global Perspective and Project Work (GPPW), an innovative subject that few education systems offer. It was a tempting opportunity for me to mentor local teachers, and unbeknownst to me, provided the opportunity (which I eagerly took) of curriculum development utilising my professional life and personal experiences in the development of Global Citizenship Education (GCE) in the 9th largest country geographically.[41,42]

GPPW is where learners broaden their outlook through the critical analysis of - and reflection on - issues of global significance. It is skills-based rather than on specific content. Learners develop research, thinking, reasoning, and communication skills by following an approach to analysing and evaluating arguments and perspectives called the critical path.[43]

The NIS system, for 18 months, utilised the Cambridge GPPW programme, it was time for the Autonomous Education Organisation of NIS (AEO) in conjunction with selected local GPPW teachers and one international teacher to reflect and begin to contextualise the programme for the Kazakhstan education programme. I was eager to promote authentic learning experiences in this programme. The GPPW programme required more direction to support teachers with the AEO goal of shifting the teaching and learning to conceptual-based learning. My background involves conceptual-based learning coupled with experience in curriculum development and assessment. I try to model myself in all situations. As teachers we are also learners, and therefore need to apply the domains of learning to ourselves and to our classroom pedagogies.

Best practice is when we educate our learners through affective practice providing cognitive mastery (cognitive domain), the head, affective engagement (affective domain), the heart and the hand (behavioural domain) related to the teachers' inner (cognitive, affective and psychomotor) conscience. The theory of transformational learning is "that learning is understood as the process of using a prior interpretation to construe a new or revised interpretation of the meaning of one's experience in order to guide future action." Frames of reference are structures of assumptions and expectations that frame an individual's tacit points of view and influence their thinking, beliefs, and actions.[44]

The NIS network aimed to develop the 21st century skills of its learners and Global Citizenship (GC) became one of the key foci of the process. Semey's GC had a strong interconnection to GPPW, advice was given by external educational advisors to implement Model United Nations (MUN)[45] and to utilise GPPW to make the connection and help develop global citizenship awareness with the learners. Also, global citizenship had recently been added to be one of Semey's school six values.[46] This is how I became involved with the AEO GPPW review.

Journey with the AEO

One early spring evening, three teachers headed across the steppe on a 14-hour overnight train journey to Astana with our prepared presentation connecting the NIS Semey strategic plan and the GPPW curricula. Our presentation led to a robust discussion. We were challenged, but with all their questions, our answers always took them back to (credible) evidence (referencing each of our points to research based evidence), either in our presentation of why we should develop GC education, to develop further the four skills (reflection, communication, critical thinking, and research) of GPPW plus embed the school values, mission statements at a deeper level, or we asked them, to answer their question by them providing the evidence - modelling the learning process (of GPPW). The challenge was when some teachers wanted answers, as if we had completed a journey and we should have the answer already, despite it being a journey that we were about to begin.

By taking our responses back to the evidence (strategic plan, research, and so on), a significant turning point for the 12 GPPW teachers for how to reflect and modify the GPPW programme occurred by taking the best of the curriculum being used at that stage considering what was happening globally in the area of global citizenship and how MUN could be embedded into GPPW. This was the beginning of a three-year partnership with the AEO for me and one Semey local colleague, mentoring the GPPW curriculum development group and assisting with teacher professional development. Along with the GPPW manager at the AEO, we worked closely together on several projects, such as teacher professional development, updating the teacher methodological guide, and the development of global citizenship within the GPPW programme. We realised that documents like the 17 Sustainable Development Goals[47] (SDG) and the Universal Declaration of Rights (UDHR)[48] had to be considered, developed, and included into the GPPW programme, and that the seven lenses (technology, culture, economics, environment, ethics, politics, and science) should be utilised more critically. We also explored pedagogy such as differentiation, how to write learning outcomes from the learning objectives. We were involved in GPPW research projects, monitoring learning outcomes, and how GPPW departments understood global issues, which helped to guide the professional development of one-week workshops led by us.

Why MUN?

MUN's purpose is to engage learners (student agency and self-directed) and allow them to develop a deeper understanding into current global issues ((re) construction of knowledge) of what is a global citizen. The four skills of GPPW - research, reflection, critical thinking, and communication - are necessary to be a successful MUN delegate. Simply, it looks at global issues, delegates research, debates (communicates) and writes a resolution (the GPPW research paper) - this is a summary of the GPPW. MUN delegates, as individual learners, construct new knowledge based upon existing and inherent knowledge. The participants (the learners) do not receive knowledge passively, but interpret what they receive through debate and resolution writing.

At NIS Semey, we researched MUN comprehensively. My knowledge of MUN was limited: two of my Grade 10 learners in a previous school had attended a MUN conference in Doha and were buzzing about the experience. Much trawling of the internet reading, making notes, dialogue with the Semey GPPW teachers and administration, establishing a comprehensive file of resources, a draft MUN action plan, and emails to organisations ensued. We learned about the New Silk Way MUN (NSWMUN) in Almaty and communicated with Dr Rafis Abazov, adjunct professor from Columbia University in New York and a visiting professor at Al Farabi National University in Almaty - this was one of his initial roles on appointment.

Late in April 2016, the train tickets were booked, my colleague, Semey's curriculum director, and I accompanied three selected Grade 10 learners to attend the 6th New Silk Way International Model United Nations[49] (NSWMUN) three-day conference in Almaty. With excitement and with some trepidation, the six of us rattled away south for 22 hours to Almaty.

It was three days of an overwhelming amount of information, observations, discussions, and the six of us came away with a greater understanding of MUN.

On day two, the three learners became delegates (learners through designing and social making), debating against university (local and international) learners, (just a few high school learners attending). They debated global issues, participated in moderated and unmoderated caucuses, and assisted in the resolution writing process (the assimilated artefact (reflection and metacognition)) and quickly began to develop an understanding of the process, the language, and to their delight, they improved their English language skills. The learners were stimulated, excited, and importantly, they had grown as learners and citizens.

The returning train journey time was utilised to reflect on the previous three days. We looked at GPPW conceptually, asking questions (5W's and H), identified what should be in the MUN action plan, how MUN could be embedded into GPPW, considered the long-term, mid-term and short-term plans, and discussed a way forward. The MUN action plan had to be connected to the school's strategic plan, the school values, GPPW learning objectives, the goals of GPPW, and the GPPW long-term plan - resulting in revising some documents. Other questions included, *"who were to be the inaugural MUN learner leaders"*? It seemed natural that these three learners should be the inaugural leaders (democratisation and agency in learner-centric education), but we would wait to see who showed the most potential, who would volunteer, and who would grow into being the MUNNISS (MUN NIS Semey) Inaugural Secretary General.

That summer of 2016, my summer break happened to be in New York city, the home of the United Nations. I took the metro from the Upper West Side to downtown New York, wondered past the Rockefeller centre and the flags of the member countries of the United Nations to 1st Avenue and 42nd Street East, and purchased my ticket to visit and tour the UN building. This helped me to gain a deeper understanding and connection to the UN. I contacted a MUN advisor (it was his full-time job) and we met for two hours over a coffee in a Starbucks near Central Park. He worked between schools in New Jersey and New York city managing MUN programmes, clubs, and conferences. I fired so many questions at him (some questions arose through the discussion at the time, some from conversations with my colleagues before coming) like, how much involvement do teachers have? Is there a strict set of rules? How strict are the protocols? Where is the head office of the MUN? How do learners attend conferences? and so on. I wrote pages of notes as I developed a greater understanding of the process, reinforcing that it was learner-led and that adults are advisors only. The New York meeting reaffirmed that my thinking was correct and we were on the correct path, but implementing it into a (GPPW) programme that all learners studied (Grade 11) was unique. He complimented us on having management that had such foresight.

Papert (1928–2016) defines constructionism as when learning happens when individuals are engaged in constructing meaningful artefacts or objects. MUN is an educational simulation and/or academic activity in which learners can learn about diplomacy, international relations, and the UN. Constructionism also shares the view of learning, which is about the building of knowledge structures through the internalisation of action over time but with attention being given to the manner of learning – also referred to as the 'art of learning' – and to understanding the relationship. MUN involves and teaches participants speaking, debating, and writing skills, in addition to critical thinking, teamwork, and leadership abilities. The key artefacts of MUN are a position paper (researched and prepared in advance based on a given global issue connected to a UN committee/organisation such as Security Council, World Health Organisation representing one of the 194 members of UN) and a conference. MUN is an active process (form) of learning: active forms of (constructionist) learning lead to improved learner attitudes and improvements in learners' thinking and communication skills (writing, oral).

How does GPPW and MUN demonstrate the five key stages of constructionism?

Table 1 highlights the connections between GPPW/MUN and constructionism.

Table 1

	Stages	Connection to GPPW and MUN
1	(Re)construction of knowledge [learners construct new understandings based on existing knowledge and actively make projects to test and refine the knowledge (and knowledge models) they are developing].	Taking of a global issue and through the critical path deconstruction, consider perspectives through the seven lenses, SDG's, UDHR and other influences.
2	Learner agency and self-directed exploration [learners take a central role in the learning process, discovering new knowledge themselves, with teachers acting as	Self-selection of global issues and research according to the seven lenses. Attendance at other MUN conferences in other cities which gives them the opportunity to practice their English skills (third language).

	facilitators and guides rather than custodians of content].	
3	Learning through designing and social making [learners are involved in designing and creating artefacts based on their own perspectives and ideas, getting feedback on their understanding not from external assessments (like exams) but from sharing their projects and artefacts with others].	Planning, organising and managing the MUN 2-day conference. The Secretary General manages the whole process Sub committees - budgeting, promotion, new friends from MUN conferences, social networking sites. Considering values.
4	Reflection and metacognition [learners use the projects and artefacts they make to reflect on their learning, gaining opportunities to consider their own learning approaches and processes as a means of facilitating understanding].	Ongoing reflection, the four skills of GPPW, the analysis of the global issue in the context of a given country and given committee/organisation. Global issues are considered at local, national, and global level.

		MUN conference debate / resolution writing and post-conference reflection.
5	Technological literacy [learners use technology to achieve specific learning goals rather than experiencing technology as a bolt-on or after-thought].	MUN lesson preparation resources, PPT's, videos, Kahoots, researching, preparation of programme, speeches, placards and so on.

Example: The GPPW programme of learning considered current global issues that were in the media (the learners chose the issue and the evidence). The learners' brief was to prepare a two to three minute referenced (media source) presentation analysing the global issue through the seven lenses. It had to be considered at local, national, and global levels, connected to the UDHR, and there needed to be consideration of how the global issue connected to the 17 SDGs. The presentation tool was through a Socratic Seminar,[50] a learner-led discussion based on Socrates' method of learner inquiry which elicits learner ownership, deep thinking, critical questioning, and a rooted sense of community. The teacher is a facilitator, but a meaningful and effective Socratic seminar occurs through intentional planning. Each learner must ask a deep question that allows the discussion to traverse across several ideas. We spent the last five minutes of the lesson writing a generalisation utilising Rolfe et al's[51] reflective model, What? So what? Now what? This was one of the methods for formative assessment. On this day, Learner Z's topic was about the North Korea and USA relationship over nuclear weapons and was to be followed with a Socratic discussion. Discussion occurred, then Learner X *"Is there anything that we can do with this global crisis"*? More debate followed - *"yes"*, *"no"*, *"maybe"*. The local teacher and I could see that the learners wanted some guidance from us. My question was: *"do you think you can do something about this global issue"*? It should be remembered that this community has experience with nuclear weapons. Learner E: *"We could prepare a video and post on social media to inform people about our views and experiences, but it must be a whole class collaborative project"*. We gave them time to consider and the answer was almost unanimous. It meant diverging from the short-term GPPW plans but we identified that the learning objectives would be covered by adapting to the learner agency and learner self-directed exploration. Those two learners who chose to be non-participants were given other GPPW work to complete. The learners planned the time plan, allocation of jobs, scripts, and the school photographer and school driver were organised to take them to the filming venue, 'The Stronger Than Death Monument', which is a sombre and impressive memorial for victims of the nuclear tests. Semipalatinsk is very close to the polygon where the Russians detonated 456 nuclear weapons. These learners, through their families and the community, have first-hand experience of people suffering from the effects of heavy radiation. Several learners in the class had been involved in a physics project for the Atom Project -an anti-nuclear movement - measuring radiation levels in Kazakhstan and presented their results at an international nuclear energy conference held in Kazakhstan. We allocated two weeks (ten lessons) for the learners to collaboratively produce a short video clip 'Global Diplomacy'[52] and create pages in social media (Facebook, Instagram, Twitter) about future leaders in a modern world.

MUN and GPPW

In the 2016 - 2017 academic year, MUN was embedded into GPPW and management were happy with our plans. There were five local Semey GPPW and one international teacher/mentor, being me. Semey GPPW teachers collaboratively refined the GPPW programme with strong leadership so that over the four terms, the programme was scaffolded as a spiral curriculum, so that the whole learning process came together in a learner-centred, learner-organised, two-day MUN conference (inaugural MUNNISS conference) from identifying and understanding self-selected global issues, to reviewing how a given country viewed a selected global issue, to the preparation of a position paper (combining the requirements of a MUN position paper and the research paper of GPPW). Each week, we were given one lesson where the MUN leaders from each GPPW class met with two GPPW teachers and the three MUN leaders. The two teachers met with the three MUN leaders to discuss the proposed leaders training lesson, taken from the long-term MUN plan and how they may mentor the leaders. The key for this process was to keep up the momentum: the GPPW staff began to follow Rogers' (1962) Law of Diffusion of Innovation [53]; one teacher quickly became a laggard and it was about change in teaching practice that suddenly involved more than just the mechanical process. Teacher X (Late Majority, Rogers (1962)) found it difficult to be a long-term team player despite support with lesson plans and activities, but his classes maintained the momentum due to the passion being developed by his MUN class leaders. Shifting and changing our mental models about what we teach, how we teach it, and how we assess learners' learning and professional growth takes some getting used to. Such changes require open-mindedness, flexibility, patience, and courage.

My role was to ensure that the GPPW learning objectives and learning outcomes were met, that the learners still gained the aims of GPPW, that the learners successfully put together a successful two-day MUN conference, and lastly for me (us) to manage the process. There was overwhelming support from management. I needed self-belief to ensure that the process was to continue and was sustainable (with ongoing refinements), and I need to work with the local teaches that also trusted the process (the early adopters /majority - Rogers (1962)) that could see the bigger vision without wanting the answers in advance.

MUN

We continued to grow the experience of MUN amongst the learners by attending the NSWMUN conferences - this time taking 32 Grade 11 learners and six Grade 10 learners who would be the foundation of the next Grade 11 leaders. We had MUN fever. The reason for taking so many learners was that it enabled a strong base for the forthcoming year, ensuring the sustainability of MUN. The second MUNNISS conference and awards from other conferences demonstrated this. How did we do this?

Each GPPW class (14) selected their own MUN leader plus a team of four who had attended the NSWMUN conference and after a few weeks one learner volunteered to be the next Secretariat General and another her deputy. Together, these two worked closely, arranging the weekly agenda for the leaders, planning each week's lesson, and began planning MUNNISS. They also found out about other MUN conferences in Kazakhstan, organising attendance for their peers at seven other MUN conferences which all involved a minimum of a 14-hour train journey.

This was an invaluable experience resulting in many measurables, such as improved language (English) skills, but also many unmeasurables, like new friendships, responsibility, citizenship, widening longer term goals, time management, confidence and so on. The Secretariat General, through her diligence, achieved a high profile amongst MUN conferences in Kazakhstan - she was selected to be on the prestigious NSWMUN Security Council where she took the award for best position paper. She was a co-organiser of a significant MUN conference in the capital where she selected delegates, prepared a manual for the topic to guide the delegates, and was co-chair with an experienced international chair. Another learner at EuroAsian MUN (university) conference, had the honour of being selected as the President of the European Union Council (competing with masters and Ph.D. students) as well as winning the Diplomacy Award. Other learners improved their communication and language skills within their class and then at MUNNISS. The 2017-2018 academic year saw refinement, a stronger MUN group of learner leaders, and the learners actively participated in their own learning. We had experience. The 2018-2019 conference will be the same.

Reflection

It is about taking opportunities, being resilient, having the support of good leadership, ongoing discussions, being passionate, gaining the support of the early adopters, and having a clear focus on self-reflection and awareness. As a lifelong learner (regardless of what curricula you are involved with, your role is within education) we should be reflecting on our practice daily, creating time for professional conversations, and being aware of what is happening globally (nationally and locally), but not just in education but politically, culturally, economically, environmentally and so on.

Chapter 20

Learning Outside of Your Comfort Zone

Dan Whiteson

It was 2011 when I began to teach. Rather than some long-held desire, it was truly much more a case of 'right place, right time' for me. I had graduated from Central Saint Martins less than a year previously and was stuck in a bit of a rut. I was working full-time in a pub while creating artwork from the living room of a shared house in my spare time. Out of the blue, a friend from my course at university contacted me, offering me the opportunity to run a weekly life drawing class in the venue where she had just become the events manager.

To put it lightly, the space was not ideal. A dark and dingy basement room in a bar on Stoke Newington Church Street, it whiffed faintly of damp and despite my best attempts, the lighting was always terrible. Unsurprisingly, I was initially reluctant; to jump into something like this with no experience felt like it could potentially be a big, embarrassing mistake, but with money getting ever tighter, and my long-held dreams of having a studio space drifting further and further from my reach, I decided to give it a go. Anything was better than the Friday night shift at a Wetherspoons, surely?

Before my first class, I felt I had a decision to make about what sort of teacher I wanted to be and how I wanted to run my classes. My own experience of creative education had been mixed at best, and certainly the life drawing classes I had attended in the past had never really satisfied me, nor attempted to build a truly creative environment in which to work. Overall, they were silent, sterile rooms in which the 'tuition' extended to a teacher walking around the room, peering over your shoulder, and telling you what you had done wrong. I rarely, if ever, made work that I was proud of in this environment, and felt there was an opportunity for me to do something truly different with my approach. Essentially, my idea was to attempt to create a class that reflected an exciting and engaging studio practice.

Perhaps the boldest and most important decision I made was that I would fully tutor the classes. Rather than tutor them in the more traditional, reactive, individual way, I talked to the students as a group and led them through several exercises, explaining thought processes and techniques as they worked. This allowed for a certain sense of anonymity among the attendees and gave me an opportunity to contribute heavily toward the tone and atmosphere of the evening. I used exercises designed to encourage freedom of expression and tried to share my enthusiasm, joy, and knowledge of drawing in the way I spoke. I did not want people to turn up to my class and feel intimidated or stifled creatively; I wanted to inspire and embolden them to make work that perhaps they never thought they could make. I wanted to wrestle life drawing away from its somewhat conservative, exclusive reputation and to open it up to anybody with even a passing interest in drawing. Whether I could do it remained to be discovered, but I felt excited at the prospect.

The first few classes were free to the public, and even once I began to charge it was only £3 to attend, which allowed me to experiment with approaches and format without feeling huge pressure or expectation from those attending. Within the first few weeks and months, I had already learned a great amount, and my passion for teaching was truly ignited. The classes were steadily building in popularity, my own confidence was growing, and a consistent structure to the sessions was beginning to emerge.

Through a combination of trialling different exercises and approaches and observing the responses of the students each week, I was able to learn quickly what the most effective and important lessons were. Perhaps the most significant realisation I had was that above all things the hardest job I had as a teacher was to get my students to *relax*. Discussion and illustration of important drawing techniques and mindset was clearly key, but if I could not encourage a sense of freedom or enjoyment in my students it was clear to me that (a) their work would suffer, (b) they were unlikely to trust me as a teacher, and (c) they were unlikely to return. I understood that if I wanted to continue to build the classes, I would need to first and foremost break through the tension and stress I was so regularly observing in many of my students, particularly those with little to no experience of life drawing (one of my key demographics in reaching a wider audience). To do this effectively, I had to work to understand what was causing this response in so many of my students. Of course, this was partly due to a lack of confidence and possibly a sense of embarrassment or of self-consciousness in response to a naked body, but what became very clear to me was that much of this response was due to learned behaviours and built in spaces outside of my classroom.

This 'pushing back' against the influence of our learned behaviours became one of the cornerstones of all my teaching. As human beings, we have built millions of habits and networks of behaviours; instinctive responses that we feel we should exhibit in certain situations. It did not take me long to realise that many of these learned behaviours are massively detrimental to a healthy approach to the creative process and so I began to explore ways of challenging my students to fight them. I knew as a practising artist that I was at my best as a creative individual when I was able to work without expectation; to take risks without fear of failure and to learn by engaging with myself, my materials or the world in new and different ways. I saw it as my greatest and most difficult task as a teacher to attempt to instil this fearlessness and freedom in my students.

After nine years of teaching tens of thousands of people from all backgrounds and experience levels, I feel confident to have found an approach and structure in my classes that allows me to cover all of the fundamental skills, both mental and technical, to enable even someone with no experience of drawing to have a fair chance at sketching the body. The exercises I use encourage attendees to avoid 'normalising' their situations, attempting to stop them from adhering to (and being restricted by) the assumptions, ideals and behaviours they perhaps feel they should be exhibiting or striving for. By placing them in positions of which they have no previous experience, they learn that taking risks, trying new things, and making mistakes are how we learn, grow our artistic language, and become more creative in our responses. The exercises themselves are not unique to my classes, but I believe how they are presented, with a running commentary explaining the reasoning behind their inclusion in terms of the technical, mental and philosophical lessons they can provide, is.

Through my experience, you can divide the main problem areas in drawing into two sections: mental and technical. Below, I have attempted to summarise the main issues as I see them.

1) Problems with mentality

A product-orientated approach

We are consistently told our time is a precious commodity. We want to make quick, 'correct' decisions and know that these choices contribute toward a 'worthy' outcome. When we attempt to apply this to drawing, we end up placing huge amounts of pressure on ourselves to make the 'right' choice all the time and to create 'good' drawings. As I explain at the beginning of all my classes, this approach is often what leads to the tension and negativity we feel towards our drawing. Rather than obsessing over making perfect, amazing things, if we can approach our task without this expectation and instead allow ourselves to enjoy all the infinite, beautiful options available to us as we engage with our materials in our own individual ways, the joy and freedom that things brings us both mentally and physically will not only allow us to enjoy the process of making so much more, but also cause us to make better work.

A narrow-minded definition of what makes a good drawing

For many, when they step into a drawing class it is very difficult to see beyond accuracy and representation being the only means to quantify their drawing skills, or to judge the quality of their work. I have seen many people become disheartened about their abilities within the first five minutes of a class, simply because they cannot perfectly reproduce the beauty of the body on their page. While technical ability is a contributing factor to the success of a drawing, when we approach our practice in this way, not only are we placing even more pressure on our shoulders, we are also shutting off many factors that actually make drawing such an exhilarating, creative and satisfying pursuit. I try to make my students see that the body, with all of its complexities and beauty, does not need to be an intimidating presence, a totem of perfection that we strive to replicate on our page, but instead an inspiration; a starting point over which to exercise our own creative impulses.

This concept extends to how we seek to understand and represent these forms too. Further to this narrow-minded definition of good drawing, we often rely on a similarly restricted approach to our *understanding* of the body. The assumption is that drawing is a single sense activity; an ability to see, to understand and then to reproduce. While this is a big part of the process, there are many alternative ways of absorbing information from our subject to allow for a more comprehensive understanding. The way I phrase it in my classes is that we can always increase the sophistication of our understanding of the world around us. How does our drawing change when we seek to *feel* a pose, or attempt to channel the emotion or character of a sitter into our own responses?

An aversion to admitting mistakes

Unfortunately, no matter how long we have been drawing, or how strong our talent may be, we will always make mistakes during the creative process. Our learned behaviours encourage us to respond negatively to our flaws and errors, and often will even push us to ignore them. It is a regular occurrence for me to see big mistakes in scale, proportion, or composition being made within the first few minutes of a drawing that are left to fester as the artist in question ignores their problems and seeks to focus instead on other more successful aspects of their drawing. By encouraging my students to not only accept mistakes as an inevitable part of their process but as a positive, necessary element of it, we can begin to challenge the preciousness we ascribe to our decisions, and to slowly build our drawing to its conclusion in a healthier way.

To help with this concept, I describe drawing as a circular process of two distinct halves, each of equal importance to the other. Part one is creative information gathering: looking, understanding, simplifying, making marks. Part two is evaluating and responding to old decisions: stopping, checking, identifying mistakes, refining. In every class I teach, I see a real imbalance in the amount of priority given to these two parts of the process. Possibly related to the issues of preciousness described above, generally people give only a very small amount of time to evaluation, which can cause major faults and inaccuracies in their work. By becoming increasingly aware of evaluation and its benefits and being able to consistently engage with it through our drawing process, we can not only better absorb our mistakes, but also create more cohesive, successful work. We prioritise structure over detail; large shapes over small shapes; simple over complex.

A need to control and normalise

Perhaps one of the biggest obstacles to one engaging with freedom and expression in our drawing practice is our instinctive responses to finding ourselves outside of our comfort zone. We search around in our brain for similar pre-existing experiences upon which we can base a response but if there is nothing there, we can feel helpless, or at a loss to react. For some of my students, just being in a life drawing class is already a position outside of their frame of reference, and I have witnessed many 'freeze' within the opening few minutes down the years.

Even for those with confidence in their drawing, this desire to control and normalise; to pull all experience back toward a place in which we feel 'safe', can be detrimental to their growth and learning as an artist. A reliance on formulas and finely honed approaches may lead to a certain level of output for established artists, but there is always more to be learned by pushing oneself outside of this safe space; to find new and different ways of solving the same problems and to allow ourselves to make work that may not be beautiful, or even good along the way, so long as we are constantly pushing ourselves to learn.

I spend a good chunk of time of each class attempting to push my students into positions out of which they must find new ways of engaging with themselves, the world, or their materials. I use change and constraint, two concepts toward which we can again instinctively baulk from, as important ways of enforcing these new approaches. Something as rudimentary as drawing with our weaker hand, or with both hands together, may initially feel foolish or pitched directly against our desire to make things of greatness, but can so often lead us to make decisions or marks that can inform our practice going forward.

2) Technical problems

Lazy observational skills

To put it bluntly, our observational skills are rubbish. Looking, understanding and absorbing information from the world around us is simply not something we spend a huge amount of time doing in our daily existence. Just walking down a busy street in London and observing those around you will show how little we visually engage with the world as human beings. Perhaps this problem has only grown in the last decade or so with the increasing influence of smartphones and other digital media. When so much of our life is spent looking at things only a few inches away from our face, maybe it has become even more challenging to learn how to look.

For those individuals who have not spent much time really *looking* at things, they can find themselves at a huge disadvantage in a life drawing class before they have even begun drawing. Therefore, I use several different exercises designed to both illustrate and challenge the problems we have with looking and speaking at length about the importance of basing all our drawing decisions on something we have *seen*. The more time I see my students giving over to observe, the more chance I know they have of being able to represent the forms in front of them.

A reliance on language to process visual information

Further to our laziness in looking, we have developed habits in processing visual information that can lead to inaccuracies in our drawing. In our everyday existence, as we look at the world around us, our brain works efficiently to fuse visual information with experience, and this allows us to define the objects we encounter with language. This means we can spend a minimal amount of time looking at things to understand the interactions and relevance of each *thing* we see. When we sit down to draw, we feel no need to challenge this process of understanding and so often I find my students spend a minuscule amount of time looking at what it is they are attempting to draw, because they have 'understood' the concept of the subject. As soon as they 'disengage' from the model, they begin to base their drawing on assumption and very quickly their work will slide further and further away from the truth of what is in front of them.

If instead we can maintain the purity of what drawing is; understanding and representing shape, line and light, and simply respond to and render these three things, we are able to become more accurate and representative in what we do. The subjective complexity of a hand becomes objectively much simpler when we can identify the squares, rectangles and circles of which it is ostensibly made. It is a simple sounding idea, but such a difficult process from which to distance ourselves, and is something I must constantly remind my students of as they work to keep them engaged with looking.

An overemphasis on details

When you combine prioritisation of accuracy and representation with a language-oriented approach to processing visual information, what can often occur is a fracturing of both our understanding and representation of the world. This instinct to compartmentalise and to assume that we must describe *everything* in our drawing causes us to narrow the focus of our observations and will often mean we end up prioritising small parts of our drawings above and beyond the success of the overall image.

I attempt to show my students that simplification of complex visual data is not only one of the most difficult things to achieve in a visual process, but also necessary to create real structure and cohesion, and to instil a real sophistication in what they do. By placing the emphasis of our process on simple, large shapes and relationships and encouraging my students to ignore unnecessary detail, they can construct much more structurally sound, successful work.

In truth, I never thought I would be teaching this long, but now the inspiration to keep going comes mainly from observing the positive effects my instruction can have on the people attending my classes regularly. However, I have also found it has become a tremendously useful tool for self-reflection and evaluation of my own practice. There have been numerous occasions in which I have caught myself falling into the traps I talk about in my teaching. Whether it is pressure to create beautiful things or catching myself making decisions based on what other people might think or like, it has been enormously useful to draw strength and confidence from the ideas and concepts I discuss in my classes.

My own practice has come a long way in the last nine years, and I think many of the decisions I have taken in terms of the direction and style of my work have been inspired by my teaching work. I was a portrait painter for several years after leaving university, but having become increasingly disillusioned with the process and feeling restricted artistically I made a decision around three years ago to completely change the focus of my work; to move away from commissioned portrait projects and instead to focus on developing my own visual language and approach. I did not think I would have had the confidence to make this choice without the experience of running my classes for all these years, and it has been really heartening and validating to develop my work alongside my students.

From that dark basement in Stoke Newington to the present day, it has truly been a privilege to work with and be inspired by the people I teach in my classes, and just like my progress as an artist and a person, my teaching is always evolving and refining. Indeed, the greatest mistake I ever made was saying yes to my friend all those years ago. If ever there was proof that stepping outside of your comfort zone can lead to wonderful, beautiful and unexpected things, then my experience over the past nine years is surely proof enough.

Conclusion

Learning Hand in Hand

Dr Catherine Speight

This volume of collected case studies considers the value of maker learning from the teacher's perspective. Each case study guides the reader through a set of processes where the learner responds to a task or opportunity in a physical way, acquiring new skills but also challenging previously held assumptions or ideas. As the book identifies, building and making are key concepts in the creation of new knowledge. For young students, knowledge that is 'all in the head' can be difficult to convey, let alone share. It can be difficult to explain something we know, when a physical representation of an idea can show others what we mean and how we came to a conclusion. Conversely, how do young people learn from verbal instruction alone? It is not the case that knowledge is transferred from the 'expert' teacher to passive and 'novice learner' but is built through experience, previously held ideas and opportunity often with the support of others. This special collection of stories, written by educators leading change in this area, helps to explain the transformative process of learning when learners have the chance to build and create physical representations of their ideas. It presents a global set of perspectives on the intricacies of the educator-learner relationship and the courage of those willing to go the extra mile for their learners.

In each chapter there are reflections on what was tried and how as well as recommendations on the use of constructionist learning in the classroom. Sometimes things did not go according to plan but in the spirit of enquiry, educators sought to make the best of an experience and its outcome and to share this with their students. In Chapter One, Anita Jantunen describes the benefits of this approach with her class offset by the pedagogical freedom she enjoys as a teacher in the Finnish school system. Unlike other countries that have modelled their educational practice on market-oriented reform, the Finnish system has managed to attain system wide success and global excellence by promoting the principles of 'equity, flexibility, creativity, teacher professionalism and trust'.[54] They have achieved this by encouraging schools to create optimal learning environments for their students and supporting individual and group-led learning. In other countries, such opportunity for free expression is limited. In Chapter Four, Ousia Foli-Bebe recalls the frustration of passively listening to lectures that had little relevance or connection to real life experience. Learning in this way can be overwhelming to the point that lessons are dreaded rather than enjoyed. Consequently, many teachers (and learners) feel the need to go alone, to innovate and create something new that is not restricted by outside intervention. The output of this process may be an idea or a physical thing. It may involve 'tinkering' or an element of play or investigation where a learner can adjust, experiment or explore with physical materials or digital code. The emphasis is not what materials you use or what you create but the ideas and skills you discover on the way. Overtime, individual educators and learners may collaborate and share their ideas with others creating communities of makers as they do. Ideas and confidence slowly improve and mastery of techniques broaden. Large groups of makers come together to create physical work spaces for their activities, sometimes these are in schools or in digital fabrication labs, or Fab Labs as they are known. While not always the choice of the individual maker or craftsperson, Fab Labs offer opportunities for digital innovation and making along with new skills and commerce. In Chapter Seven, Guiako Obin describes the challenges of setting up a 'Baby (Fab) Lab' in Abobo, one of the poorest boroughs of the Ivory Coast, Africa. The aim of the lab was to create opportunities for girls and young women to practise physical science and to learn digital skills set against a complex and at times dangerous geopolitical landscape. Obin attributes the success of the 'Baby Lab' to the local people who support it and its ethos of putting the well-being of the girls and young women that use it at its core. In Russia, Andrey Guryev shares similar reflections on building a STEAM lab from scratch. Like Obin's experience, Guryev describes the success of the lab as owing to the flexibility of the community that supports it. In his lab, young children are introduced to creative problem solving from an early age. When they reach the age of 16 they are given additional business and entrepreneurial support that helps some go onto to establish creative businesses.

Other authors in this volume attribute the success of physical learning to other means. Dance teacher and pedagogue, Alison Swann presents a fascinating insight into the role of embodied learning. Swann describes the initial reticence she encountered from some teachers who thought learning through dance was about counting to time or moving to a beat. It was only when she described how dance could be used to express ideas and concepts and where children were free to respond bodily that her colleagues understood. Her work and research began to evolve from children learning to 'dance the words' to then 'learn physically' and then 'learn physically and interactively'. She now uses dance as a multi-sensory approach to learning: "If we embody something, if we learn through doing and making dance, learning is deeper and longer-lasting. It quite literally is 'in our bodies'" (Swann). Like physical making with our hands or planning code with our brains, learning whole bodied creates opportunity for transformative engagement that is memorable and stays with us long after the lesson.

Many contributors to this volume have been inspired by the ideas of mathematician, scientist and educator

Seymour Papert. His views, shaped initially by constructivist thought, are about creating knowledge with our hands as a way of demonstrating process and understanding, what he called constructionism. As his ideas evolved, he valued the role of collaboration in knowledge building and problem solving as well as the importance of context and the teacher as a guided participant. His mission to transform the learning environment continues apace with many teachers throughout the world changing the face of education by building constructionist learning classrooms. When we make or build, we invest in ourselves, we work out problems or solutions, we transfer cognitive ideas into physical models. In the classroom, constructionist learning is about helping children and young people to work out ideas for themselves and to build a collaborative learning environment where opportunities to play, test and experiment are par for the course. The notion of 'thinking with one's hands' is about the construction and physical manifestation of knowledge through this process. While it may seem obvious, the act of making is a universally prevalent way of understanding the world. This shift in understanding has been driven by technological change and advancement but it is also about harnessing change in the relationships we have with others, beginning with the classroom. This means acknowledging the pivotal role of the educator, providing them with the support and materials they need to deliver learning but most importantly giving them the freedom to construct what that learning should be. The many successful stories in this book present what happens when educators (and learners) are given the opportunity to be innovative and to think independently without jurisdiction or government measurement.

Contributors

Foreword: Why Learn by Making? - Dr William Rankin

Dr William Rankin is the Founding Learning & Educational Technology Designer at Unfold Learning, and an educator with broad experience in educational technologies. He served as the Director of Learning on the global education team at Apple Inc. He recently completed an appointment as Director of Learning and Research for pi-top. For more than 25 years, he has worked with schools, governments, and learning organisations to design, develop, and implement innovative learning programmes that use real-world projects to break out of the confines of the classroom, equipping learners with the experience and fusion skills they'll need to succeed in the third millennium.

Introduction: Farida Danmeri

Farida Danmeri has extensive experience in teaching, STEAM education, research, curriculum development and teacher training in international environments. Farida is the editor of A Year of Making and Learning.

Chapter 1: Implementing P4C in the Secondary Classroom - Anita Jantunen

Anita Jantunen currently works at the University of Helsinki as project planner in the Culturally and Linguistically Aware Basic Education project at the Centre for Educational Assessment. She has worked as a secondary school subject teacher and as a vice principal. She graduated from an international MBA programme in educational leadership in 2019. She is a PhD candidate and her research topic concerns the leadership of diverse school communities. Through her work as a researcher, she wishes to promote equality and equity in education.

Chapter 2: Developing Self-Learning Communities to Promote Social and Tech Innovations in Making - Xavier Auffret, Romain Chanut & Justine Hannequin

Xavier Auffret is a French designer-engineer specialised in innovation through design. He is a co-founder of L'Atelier Universel, a recognised multidisciplinary innovation and design consultancy. He leads foresight and research & development projects for industry, health and research institutes. In addition to his design practice, he regularly gives lectures to sensitise new audiences to design. Xavier is one of the co-designers, with Laure Guillou and Chemsedine Herriche, of Jerry, the do-it-yourself open source computer and one of the founding members of the association that is currently spreading the project around the world: Jerry Do It Together (DIT).

Romain Chanut has a Master's degree in Information System Management, this cooperative entrepreneur co-founded the DIT initiative to offer an alternative vision of IT that is respectful of humans and our planet. He acts as the role of spokesperson and facilitator of online discussions, while designing and organising the educational workshops that are at the heart of the international development of the Jerry DIT movement. He is passionate about the Internet, communication and sociology.

Justine Hannequin joined the Jerry community in 2012. She has contributed to the creation of workshop formats, and the evolution of the visual identity of the project. After participating in open source environments, fablabs and hackerspaces in France and Europe, she obtained a Master's degree in Educational Technology at the Centre for Research and Interdisciplinarity in Paris. A designer by training, she has been freelancing since 2011. She currently designs and draws ergonomic and educational digital products.

Chapter 3: Developing International Networks of Innovation - David Li

In 2010, David Li co-founded XinCheJian, the first hackerspace in China to promote hacker/maker culture and open source hardware. In 2011, he co-founded Hacked Matter, a research hub on the maker movement and open innovation. In 2015, he co-founded Maker Collider, a platform to develop the next generation IoT from the

Maker community. He is also the executive director of the Shenzhen Open Innovation Lab which facilitates collaboration between global smart hardware entrepreneurs and Shenzhen Open Innovation ecosystem.

Chapter 4: Launching an EcoTecLab: Empowering Communities in Togo - Ousia Foli-Bebe

Ousia A. Foli-Bebe is a Togolese innovator. He initially trained in Environment and Renewable Energies. He is the Founder and Executive Manager of EcoTecLab makerspace, where he trains and empowers youth through innovation and tinkering. With his maker experience, Ousia co-designed and built the MoLab, a mobile STEAM Laboratory (https://www.molab-project.org/). With the Molab he has been spreading STEM in Togo, village to village.

Chapter 5: Investigating the Greatness of the Past - Camila Cerezo & Malena Cerezo

Camila Cerezo studied Demography and Tourism in 1995 at the Kennedy University in Buenos Aires. She began working as an English teacher at the Instituto Esteban Agustín Gascón in 1999. Her passion for arts and crafts led her to pursue studies in fashion at the Escuela Normal Superior N° 6 in 2006. She is currently completing her degree in Primary School Teaching. She has now combined her two passions: teaching and crafting, by working as a technology and crafts teacher at the Instituto Esteban Agustín Gascón.

Malena Cerezo finished law school at the University of Buenos Aires. She stayed on to teach at the same university for over 14 years. She finished her Master's in Global Rule of Law and Constitutional Democracy in Genova, Italy in 2012. In 2010, she became a member of the leadership team of the Instituto Esteban A.Gascón primary school in Buenos Aires. The school has an innovative programme of study. She is currently finishing her primary school teaching degree and psychology degree.

Chapter 6: Dance as a Multi-Sensory Approach to Learning - Alison Swann

Alison Swann is a Dance in Education Specialist with over 30 years of experience. She trained at Trinity Laban in Contemporary Technique and Movement Analysis. She took her Cert.Ed at Goldsmiths College London University and has taught in schools and worked with education authorities across the UK. Alison is a director of Dance Educates Ltd., a consultancy focusing on dance in schools and using movement as a multi-sensory approach to learning.

Chapter 7: The Birth of the Baby Lab - Guiako Obin

Guiako Obin is the Executive Director of the Ivorian Fab Lab Baby Lab. He assists companies on digital transformation issues, and develops digital social inclusion programmes for organisations. Baby Lab, is the first Ivorian Fab Lab enrolled in the worldwide network of the Massachusetts Institute of Technology, whose vision is to make neighbourhoods potential technological innovation hubs. Guiako is a distinguished ambassador representing the Ivory Coast in the Next Einstein Forum programme of the African Institute of Sciences and Mathematics.

Chapter 8: Starting a STEM Lab from Scratch - Andrey Guryev

Andrey Guryev is the Founder and head of the Laboratory of Robotics and High Technology ASLab in which children, students and teachers are trained in areas of modern engineering. He developed a multi-level robotics and design curriculum aimed at developing imagination, fine motor skills, cognitive and creative abilities, during experiments and research in classes. He recently launched the science educational channel ASLab Media, for students, parents and teachers who are interested in robotics and technology.

Chapter 9: Tracing the Development of the 'Innovation Master Class with LEGO Mindstorms EV3' for Warwick Manufacturing Group (WMG) at the University of Warwick - Dr Ali Ahmad

Dr Ali Ahmad is a Senior Fellow of the Higher Education Academy and module leader for Innovation at the Warwick Manufacturing Group, University of Warwick. He has an MSc in Information Systems from the London School of Economics, an MSc in Management Research from the University of Oxford's Said Business School and a PhD in Entrepreneurship from Dublin City University. He has experience in teaching and scholarship in the areas of entrepreneurship and innovation.

Chapter 10: Project-Based Learning: A Transdisciplinary Learning Experience - Mala Sinha

Mala Sinha has a Bachelor's degree in Biology and a Master's in Anthropology from The University of Delhi, India. She has had varied experiences of delivering American, British and IB curricula in US and Indian schools, respectively. She has taught in culturally and ethnically diverse classrooms with students with varied levels of English proficiency as well as special needs. Currently, she is teaching IB Diploma Program Biology and Environment Systems in an international school in India.

Chapter 11: Make Your School: A Creative Tech Workshop - Elena Tibi

Elena Tibi is the project leader of Make Your School at Wissenschaft im Dialog gGmbH since the project began in 2016. Beforehand, she built up and coordinated the project Debate Science! European Student Parliaments. Elena started her professional career at the European teacher's association Science on Stage. She has also developed and guided educational workshops for children at Autostadt GmbH, the communications platform of the Volkswagen Group.

Chapter 12: Establishing a Fablab: Fostering Local Creativity - Martin Oloo

Martin Oloo is the Founder and Managing Director of Fablab Winam, where he provides a platform for makers, engineers, students, artists, and artisans to unleash their dreams through sharing and building with the help of digital fabrication tools. He supports upcoming innovators and curious creative individuals to build models that can be scaled to market through his Fablab.

Chapter 13: Designing Open Learning Challenges - Jenny Kostka

Jenny Kostka received her Bachelor's degree in Physics with a concentration in secondary education, and has taught high school science in public, private, and charter school settings. She has over 12 years of teaching experience. In 2014, she completed a Master's programme in Technology, Innovation, and Education at the Harvard Graduate School of Education. Since that year, she has worked as a teacher at the South Shore Charter Public School and at the Tremont School, as a technology integration specialist at SSCPS, and as a learning designer at pi-top.

Chapter 14: Developing the Research Skills of Pupils - Marina Gardash

Marina Gardash studied at the Slavyansk Chemical and Mechanical Technical School, where she received an engineering and technology diploma. She continued her studies at the Ukrainian Engineering and Pedagogical Academy. In 2005, she received a Master's degree in Vocational Training. She began teaching at the Engineering College of the Donbass State Engineering Academy as a teacher of chemistry and ecology in 2007. She is now a teacher of chemistry and biology at Kramatorsk Higher Professional School.

Chapter 15: Taking Risks: The Transformative Power of Agency - Mark Rasi

Mark Rasi is an Australian education professional with over 20 years of leadership experience in P-12 schools. His career has consisted of appointments to executive positions in a P-12 independent school; 14 years as a curriculum leader in two independent schools; an adjunct lecturer at The University of Queensland and university partner at Queensland University of Technology. Mark has been involved in creating and implementing innovative teaching practices and learning environments within the classroom and across the whole school.

Chapter 16: Motivating Students to Solve Community Problems - Girish Nair

Girish Nair is the Founder & CEO of Curiosity Gym. Prior to founding Curiosity Gym, he was the CEO of Netcore, one of India's leading email and mobile technology platform service providers and also a Partner at Tandem Capital a Silicon Valley based seed capital fund where he mentored entrepreneurs. He has a Bachelor's in Engineering from IIT Bombay, a Master's in Industrial Engineering from Virginia Tech and also studied Engineering Management at Stanford. Curiosity Gym aims to create a platform for young people and adults to have fun while learning.

Chapter 17: Living History Experiences - Lynn Hannay

Lynn Hannay spent 38 years in primary education in both inner-city state and independent sectors. She co-founded The Lyceum school in Central London which offered high academic standards alongside an education rich in the performing and visual arts. She chaired The National Association of Primary Education for 4 years, and is the author of "Go Teach KS2" a guide to teaching maths and English outside the classroom.

Chapter 18: Constructionist Modification of the NASA Touchdown Lander Lesson - Nick Giacobbe & Brandon Rodriguez

As the son of two special educators, Nick Giacobbe grew up with a passion for inclusive education and a dream to follow in their footsteps. For more than a dozen years, Nick has worked in the Chicago Public Schools as a special education teacher. He has provided professional development for the Illinois Digital Educators Alliance, Rochelle Lee Teacher Award program, the Chicago Area Reading Association, and the Chicago Public Schools among others.

Brandon Rodriguez presently works at NASA Jet Propulsion Lab as a STEM Education Specialist. After a rewarding career in research, he wanted to share his love of science with the next generation. He became a high school science teacher and has since joined the University of California - Riverside as part of a partnership with NASA in order to work with teachers on bringing exciting science into classrooms nationwide.

Chapter 19: Achieving Sustainable Transformative Learning: Reflections on Educational Adventures in Kazakhstan - Sue Parkes

Currently, Sue Parkes is undertaking her Doctorate in Education at the University of Canterbury, Christchurch, New Zealand, her topic is "Global Competency: discourse within the New Zealand education curricula". Prior to this, she was an international teacher for eight years. Her last posting was for four years in Kazakhstan, where she mentored Kazakh teachers.

Chapter 20: Learning Outside of your Comfort Zone - Dan Whiteson

Dan Whiteson is a figurative painter and teacher living and working in London. His work has been shown in numerous solo and group shows across the UK and Europe, and can be found in private collections all over the world. His newer work deals with the impact of the digital age on human physicality.

Conclusion: Learning Hand in Hand - Dr Catherine Speight

Dr Catherine Speight is the V&A Research Institute (VARI) Research and Teaching Fellow. Catherine has worked at the interface of different disciplines and sectors, developing hybrid research models to understand the value and significance of learning appropriate to different contexts and audiences in museums, universities and schools. Catherine's current passion is examining the making process and what it means to be a maker.

Acknowledgements

We would like to thank everyone who has supported the making of this book.

Thank you to all of the international educators who shared their stories of making and learning.

Thank you to all who have supported the educational projects mentioned in this book.

Notes

Chapter 1: Implementing P4C in the Secondary Classroom - Anita Jantunen

1. The Finnish National Agency of Education. (2014). National Core Curriculum for Basic Education.

2. Sahlberg, P. (2011). Finnish lessons: what can the world learn from educational change in Finland. Teachers College Press: New York.

3. Philosophy for Children. (2019). https://p4c.com/ [Accessed 12 December 2019].

4. SeeSaw. (2019). https://web.seesaw.me/ [Accessed 12 December 2019].

Chapter 2: Developing Self-Learning Communities to Promote Social and Tech Innovations in Making - Xavier Auffret, Romain Chanut & Justine Hannequin

5. Adopt a Jerry. (2019). www.adoptajerry.cc [Accessed 12 December 2019].

Chapter 3: Developing International Networks of Innovation - David Li

6. British Council. (2016). Hello Shenzhen - meet the Shenzhen makers.

https://creativeconomy.britishcouncil.org/blog/17/02/16/ hello-shenzhen-meet-shenzhen-makers/ [Accessed 12 December 2019].

Chapter 4: Launching an EcoTecLab: Empowering Communities in Togo - Ousia Foli-Bebe

7. Mwaura,W. (2018). Les innovateurs togolais transforment les déchets du monde en robots https://www.bbc.com/afrique/region-46386287 [Accessed 12 December 2019].

Chapter 5: Investigating the Greatness of the Past - Camila Cerezo & Malena Cerezo

8. Institutogascon. (2019). http://www.institutogascon.com.ar/ [Accessed 12 December 2019].

9. Astrolab Motion. (2016). ¿Quieres saber quiénes fueron los mayas? (Reporteros de la Historia). https://www.youtube.com/watch?v=wq4oeeMdptU [Accessed 12 December 2019].

Chapter 6: Dance As a Multi-Sensory Approach to Learning - Alison Swann

10. The Place. (2019). https://www.theplace.org.uk/ [Accessed 12 December 2019].

11. The Place. (2010). Learn Physical interactive evaluation: Autumn and Spring term, 2009/2010. https://www.theplace.org.uk/sites/default/files/downloads/LearnPhysical%20Interactive%20Evaluation.pdf [Accessed 12 December 2019].

Chapter 8: Starting a STEM Lab from Scratch - Andrey Guryev

12. ASLab Media. (2019). https://www.youtube.com/channel/UCTgdlRfTsjmH7kn9tCva6DQ [Accessed 12 December 2019].

Chapter 9: Tracing the Development of the 'Innovation Master Class with LEGO Mindstorms EV3' for Warwick Manufacturing Group (WMG) at the University of Warwick - Dr Ali Ahmad

13. Moodle. (2019). https://moodle.org/ [Accessed 12 December 2019].

Chapter 10: Project-Based Learning: A Transdisciplinary Learning Experience - Mala Sinha

14. PBLWorks. (2019). https://www.pblworks.org/what-is-pbl/gold-standard-project-design [Accessed 12 December 2019].

15. Curry, A. (2015). Mercury in San Francisco Bay.

https://ww2.kqed.org/quest/2015/11/05/mercury-in-san-francisco-bay/ [Accessed 12 December 2019].

Chapter 11: Make Your School: A Creative Tech Workshop - Elena Tibi

16. Fraillon, J., Schulz, W., John. A., (2013). International computer and information literacy study 2013: Assessment framework. IEA: Amsterdam.

17. Make Your School. (2019). Materials. www.makeyourschool.de/material [Accessed 12 December 2019].

18. Hirschmann, K./Wissenschaft im Dialog. (2019). Brainstorming on how to overcome the challenges.

19. Hirschmann, K./Wissenschaft im Dialog. (2019). The hacking.

20. Kopatz, G./Wissenschaft im Dialog. (2019). Group presentations.

Chapter 12: Establishing a Fablab: Fostering Local Creativity - Martin Oloo

21. Fab Academy. (2019). www.fabacademy.org [Accessed 12 December 2019].

22. Fab Foundation. (2019). www.fabfoundation.org [Accessed 12 December 2019].

Chapter 13: Designing Open Learning Challenges - Jenny Kostka

23. Kostka, J. (2019). Post-exam project description & rubric. https://drive.google.com/file/d/1sVAHiNA447ldlePKht7t S5rH9YNVeY67/view [Accessed 12 December 2019].

24. Instructables. (2019). https://www.instructables.com/ [Accessed 12 December 2019].

25. Make. (2019). https://makezine.com/projects/ [Accessed 12 December 2019].

26. Thingiverse. (2019). https://www.thingiverse.com/ [Accessed 12 December 2019].

27. Blockposters. (2019).https://www.blockposters.com/create/ [Accessed 12 December 2019].

Chapter 15: Taking Risks: The Transformative Power of Agency - Mark Rasi

28. Herrington, J., Reeves, T. C., and Oliver, R. (2010). A guide to authentic e-learning. London: Routledge.

Chapter 17: Living History Experiences - Lynn Hannay

29. Horsler, V. (2003). Living in the Past, Weidenfeld and Nicolson for English Heritage.

30. Kentwell Hall. (2019). http://www.kentwell.co.uk/ [Accessed 12 December 2019].

31. Association for Living History, Farm and Agricultural Museums

(ALHFAM). (2019).www.alhfam.org [Accessed 12 December 2019].

32. Anderson, J. (1984) Time-machines: The world of living history, American Association for State and Local History: Tennessee.

33. Hales, S. (1986). 'The primary school experience' in Woodhead S. And Tinniswood, A. (Eds) (1986) No Longer Dead to Me, National Trust.

34. Thibault, M. (2007). Bring history to life with a living history day,

https://www.ncpedia.org/anchor/anchor [Accessed 12 December 2019].

35. Freshwater Theatre Company. (2019). www.freshwatertheatre.co.uk [Accessed 12 December 2019].

36. Horsler, V. (2003). Living in the Past, Weidenfeld and Nicolson for English Heritage.

Chapter 18: Constructionist Modification of the NASA Touchdown Lander Lesson - Nick Giacobbe & Brandon Rodriguez

37. Jet Propulsion Laboratory (2019). Touchdown. https://www.jpl.nasa.gov/edu/teach/activity/touchdown/ [Accessed 12 December 2019].

38. Seesaw. (2019). https://web.seesaw.me/ [Accessed 12 December 2019].

39. Resnick, M. (2017). Lifelong kindergarten: Cultivating creativity through projects, passion, peers, and play. The MIT Press: Massachusetts.

Chapter 19: Achieving Sustainable Transformative Learning: Reflections on Educational Adventures in Kazakhstan - Sue Parkes

40. Nazarbayev Intellectual Schools. (2019). http://nis.edu.kz/en/ [Accessed 12 December 2019].

41. Oxfam. (2019). What is global citizenship? https://www.oxfam.org.uk/education/who-we-are/what-is-global-citizenship [Accessed 12 December 2019].

42. UNESCO. (2014). Global citizenship education: preparing learners for the challenges of the 21st century. https://unesdoc.unesco.org/ark:/48223/pf0000227729 [Accessed 12 December 2019].

43. Cambridge Assessment International Education. (2019). www.cambridgeinternational.org [Accessed 12 December 2019].

44. Taylor, E. (2008). Transformative learning theory. New Directions for Adult and

Continuing Education, 119, 5-15.

45. Best Delegate. (2007). What is Model United Nations?

https://bestdelegate.com/what-is-model-united-nations/ [Accessed 12 December 2019].

46. Council of International Schools. (2019). Global citizenship & your school.

https://www.cois.org/for-schools/educating-for-global-citizenship [Accessed 12 December 2019].

47. The United Nations. (2019). About the sustainable development goals.

https://www.un.org/sustainabledevelopment/sustainable-development-goals/

[Accessed 12 December 2019].

48.Youth for Human Rights. (2019). United Nations Universal Declaration of Human

Rights https://www.youthforhumanrights.org/what-are-human-rights/universal-

declaration-of-human-rights/articles-1-15.html [Accessed 12 December 2019].

49. Al-Farabi Kazakh National University. (2019). Model UN New Silk Way Home

Page. http://munnsw.kz/ [Accessed 12 December 2019].

50. Davenport, M. (2016). Socratic seminars: Building a culture of student-led

discussion https://www.edutopia.org/blog/socratic-seminars-culture-student-led-

discussion-mary-davenport [Accessed 12 December 2019].

51. University of Cumbria. (2006). Rolfe et al.'s (2001) reflective model

https://my.cumbria.ac.uk/media/MyCumbria/Documents/ReflectiveModelRolfe.pdf

[Accessed 12 December 2019].

52. NIS Semey, Kazakhstan. (2017). The art of global diplomacy.

https://www.youtube.com/watch?v=FNCUE4QGVaY. [Accessed 12 December 2019].

53. Rogers, E. (1962). Diffusion of Innovations. Free Press of Glencoe.

Conclusion: Learning Hand in Hand - Catherine Speight

54. Sahlberg, P. (2007). Education policies for raising student learning: the Finnish approach, Journal of Education Policy, 22:2, 147-171, DOI: 10.1080/02680930601158919

Printed in Great Britain
by Amazon